Insight Coaching & Mentoring Programme

Understanding Coaching & Mentoring

INSIGHT COACHING & MENTORING
Richard Hale & Eileen Hutchinson

Insight Coaching & Mentoring Programme

British Library Cataloguing in Publication Data

A catalogue record for this book is available from the British Library.

ISBNs Paperback 9781780921082,ePub 9781780921099, PDF 9781780921105

© 2009, 2012 Richard Hale and Eileen Hutchinson. All rights reserved.

Version 0.3 011211

MX Publishing, 335 Princess Park Manor, Royal Drive, London, N11 3GX.

www.mxpublishing.co.uk

Cover design by Daniel Bailey

www.ravenanimations.co.uk

Insight Coaching & Mentoring Programme

Workbook and programme outline

This programme will give you the opportunity to learn and practice new skills and techniques in order to improve your performance both as a coach and mentor. The programme consists of several Modules covering different aspects of coaching and mentoring, with the aim of balancing the provision of knowledge with exercises and tools to support you in practice as a coach or mentor. Whilst the overall objective is to facilitate your professional development, we also aim to provide a balance with underpinning and thought-provoking research. We draw on the research of others, and in line with academic convention, acknowledge and reference their work, and we provide materials and findings drawn from our own specialist research.

Accreditation Options

The material from the Insight Modules may be used to support you on an accredited programme under an agreement between our partner Value Improvement Projects held with Middlesex University, Institute for Work Based Learning. Specifically we are able to offer accredited options at undergraduate and postgraduate levels. Completion of accredited modules using these support materials leads upon successful assessment, to issue of an accreditation certificate from Middlesex University. Credits may be used as a route into Middlesex University qualifications at undergraduate and postgraduate level up to Masters degree. If you are following this accredited route then the Insight Modules are provided alongside educational support and assessment from qualified academic supervisors.

Institute of Leadership and Management (ILM)

The *Insight Coaching & Mentoring Programme* is endorsed by the ILM and as such is recognised as a programme which includes assessment. The material in the Insight Modules has been cross- referenced with the ILM national standards linked to the Qualification and Credit Framework and may be used in conjunction with the following programmes:

The ILM Level 3 Award in Workplace Coaching for Team Leaders and First Line Managers which focuses on the skills and knowledge required to coach team members effectively in the workplace and develop their performance. For individuals looking to develop their careers as workplace coaches the ILM Level 3 Certificate for Professional Workplace Coaches.

The Level 5 Certificate in Coaching and Mentoring in Management which is aimed at managers responsible for coaching/mentoring newly-appointed managers, professional/senior technical staff. For those wishing to develop their careers as professional management the Diploma for Professional Management Coaches and Mentors.

The ILM Level 7 Certificate in Executive Coaching and Leadership Mentoring (QCF) which is aimed at senior managers who want to develop a coaching style of leadership in their organisation, or training professionals seeking to provide coaching support to develop leadership capability in others. For those who wish to develop their careers as executive coaches the Diploma for Professional Executive Coaches and Leadership Mentors.

Insight Coaching & Mentoring Programme

CONTENTS

Insight Coaching & Mentoring Programme

1 - Objectives

1.1 – By the end of this workbook you will be able to...

- Describe the purpose of mentoring
- Understand a range of definitions and types of coaching
- Differentiate between coaching and mentoring
- Differentiate between cultural difference in definitions of mentoring
- Recognise some of the skills common to both coaching and mentoring
- Understand the benefits of coaching and mentoring
- Describe your own experiences as a coach or mentor
- Understand the context of coaching and mentoring compared to other development interventions
- Use The Wheel of Life as a tool to explore personal values
- Understand some of the key research that has been conducted into the dynamics of mentoring relationships

Consider the above objectives and your personal goals in completing this Module. Make a note of the outcomes you would like to achieve in terms of knowledge, skills or insights you are seeking.

Insight Coaching & Mentoring Programme

1.2 – ILM Unit Cross Referencing

Title:	Reviewing own ability as a management coach or mentor		Unit Ref:	D5.02
Learning outcomes **The learner will**	**Assessment criteria** **The learner can (in an organisation with which they are familiar)**			
1 - Review the effect of own value systems and ability to deal with performance problems on own coaching and mentoring behaviour	1.1	Review own ethical and moral views, beliefs, attitudes and values and their effect on own coaching and mentoring practice		
	1.2	Review own ability to address poor or inappropriate attitudes, behaviours and workplace relationships and its effect on own coaching and mentoring practice		

Title:	Critically reviewing the role of the leadership mentor or executive coach in developing leadership performance		Unit Ref:	D7.01
Learning outcomes **The learner will**	**Assessment criteria** **The learner can (in an organisation with which they are familiar)**			
1 - Evaluate the contribution of leadership mentoring and executive coaching in developing leadership performance	1.1	Appraise the abilities and performance characteristics of effective leaders		
	1.2	Evaluate alternative strategies for developing leadership performance and the potential contribution of leadership mentoring and executive coaching to individual and organisational performance		
2 - Critically review the necessary conditions for leadership mentoring and executive coaching to develop effective leadership practice	2.1	Critically review the purpose and role of leadership mentoring and executive coaching		
	2.2	Critically review the characteristics of and conditions for effective leadership mentoring and executive coaching practice		
	2.3	Critically review the skills and behaviours required for effective performance in the leadership mentoring and executive coaching role		

Insight Coaching & Mentoring Programme

Title:	Critically reviewing own ability to perform effectively as a leadership mentor or executive coach	Unit Ref:	D7.02

Learning outcomes The learner will	Assessment criteria The learner can (in an organisation with which they are familiar)	
2 - Understand how the client's personal characteristics and organisational skills affects own performance as leadership mentor or executive coach	2.1	Explain how client's personalities, characters, value systems, knowledge, skills, experience, role and organisational context affects leadership mentoring or executive coaching practice

> *Considering the Institute of Leadership and Management learning outcomes above, make a note of which outcomes and criteria are particularly relevant for your personal development.*

Insight Coaching & Mentoring Programme

2 - Introduction to Coaching and Mentoring

2.1 – Authors' Perspectives - Understanding Coaching and Mentoring

Dr Richard Hale

 I had spent many years running face-to-face training programmes related to behavioural issues such as interpersonal skills, impact and influence and leadership. As a trainer I had learnt how to satisfy the participants and the clients by ensuring they felt they had learnt a lot at the end of a programme. Usually this was evidenced by completion of a post-course evaluation questionnaire which asked questions such as: 'Do you feel you have learnt a lot from the programme?' However, over time I had become more sceptical as to what people who reported learning, had actually learnt. I wondered whether they had made sustainable changes to their behaviour, and how they would fare with their new skills in the 'real world'.

Some of my initial research did show that where we had over 90 per cent of participants reporting having changed at the end of a course, when we went back to them after one year, only around six per cent said they had managed to sustain that change and embed it into their behaviour. For instance people who had developed skills of assertiveness in the classroom found in their organisation that it was a real challenge to implement those skills. One reason was that other people found it difficult to accept the change, the 'new person', and would push them back to being the 'old person' they knew and understood. I became interested in the idea that mentoring could provide a missing link between the training course, where the skills are developed, and the real world where change needed to happen. I also realised much had been written about mentoring, organisations were setting up mentoring schemes and it was generally seen as a good thing to do, however there was limited grounded research into mentoring in the organisational context.

In particular there was little research into what made for a good mentoring relationship. So I set out to research the dynamics of mentoring, with the naive idea that I might be able to create a formula for successfully matching mentors and mentees. I studied the literature and I interviewed many mentors and mentees in corporate organisations to try to scratch beneath the surface of their mentoring relationships. Whilst I haven't found the magic formula, I did discover other things, and many of these findings are summarised in the article in this workbook and many of the outcomes from the research have been incorporated into material and tools throughout this programme.

So is mentoring the missing link between courses and real learning? In some ways I think it is. For instance mentoring can take people beyond just the acquisition of skills.

A good mentor will:

- help the mentee to explore how and when to implement skills
- encourage them to move from thinking about doing something to actually doing it
- encourage personal reflection on actions taken.

Insight Coaching & Mentoring Programme

I have been fortunate enough to work with some very talented people from a range of different backgrounds over the years, and some merit special mention here. In my doctoral research I was under the supervision of Dr Alan Mumford, renowned as the co-author of much work in the field of learning styles. I explored in my research the link between learning styles and mentoring, and the findings are included in these materials. I recall as a student being taught to categorise learning into the headings of knowledge, skills and attitudes and that a challenge for trainers has always been how to address the issue of changing or developing attitudes in others. Alan suggested instead of attitudes I should pursue the line of learning 'insights', as he felt that mentoring could be a means of helping facilitate significant learning in terms of insights. Indeed I did pursue this in my research and you will see later, in the article and in the programme, reference to how I was able to categorise insights. I think this is a much neglected aspect of learning and one which merits further research.

In recent years I have been working with Alan Chambers MBE, the polar adventurer who led the first successful unsupported British expedition to the Geographic North Pole. Alan was recognised for demonstrating 'exceptional leadership in extreme adversity' and it is clear that his approach to coaching and mentoring his team was a critical determinant of his success. I have also been working with Phil Davies, former Welsh rugby union international and successful coach in the field of elite sports at international level. A core message from Phil is the importance of talent identification and development. I have incorporated key thinking from Alan and Phil in my work and in this programme you will see some reference to their approach to coaching and mentoring.

Additionally I have been working with my co-author in this series, Eileen Hutchinson, who has developed highly successful and innovative approaches to coaching and mentoring in the field of mental health. We have created this programme in order to bring you a research and practitioner based resource, drawing the best from these worlds of business, healthcare and sport. See www.eileenhutchinson.com

Contact HCMA for further details www.hcma.me.uk

Insight Coaching & Mentoring Programme

Eileen Hutchinson

 Over the past fifteen years I have worked within the field of personal development, education and employment with groups of people who were considered disadvantaged, and suffered with a multitude of personal and behavioural issues. In March 2000 I featured in a documentary commissioned by Probation Services for the pioneering work I have done with ex-offenders, which was shown nationally.

My experience of working with people who were labelled with a mental health problem informs me that effective learning is driven by individuals, and when individuals have an element of control over the learning experience the outcome becomes more potent. My methodology is process-driven while encouraging the peer learning model. The peer learning model is very powerful as it combines a focus on individual needs, with support from co-learners that can lead to mutually beneficial and lasting results

During the past three years my pioneering specialist mentoring and coaching programmes have been piloted within the mental health sector. The context of the peer-to-peer learning programmes include mentoring, coaching and NLP techniques, delivered to a mixed group of staff, volunteers and service users. These peer-to-peer learning programmes are the first training programmes to be accredited by ILM - The Institute of Leadership and Management. We are now evaluating the effectiveness of our mentoring models by assessing the impact they are having on the people involved. This programme is being described as transformational.

I run a widely recognised Coaching and NLP Practice with Centre status from the Institute of Leadership and Management (see www.i-l-m.com) and I have undertaken research on peer mentoring for the University of Hertfordshire Recovery Centre. I employ various teaching training techniques and use some traditional methods which are essentially trainer-centered. My style is very informal and delivered in a relaxed process format. For me learning is an ongoing process and there is always something new to learn and I believe each one of us is unique; therefore I focus on people's individuality to help them design their life. I work with and receive mentoring and coaching from some very talented people, namely: trained by Sue Knight, an international NLP Master trainer; working with Mark Straker who has achieved a major film accolade for the 'One of Us' film project which he wrote and produced.

I seek to enhance our communities with people of integrity, compassion and enthusiasm for life, who in a holistic way can be of service to others.

Human flowering is the poetry of the ongoing passage of growth and development, inspiring change and enlightenment. Our vulnerability leads to humility, which leads to open-mindedness. As a consequence, this leads inevitably to learning. Throughout our lives we seek people who can pass onto us another way of seeing the world and now I have the pleasure of working with my co-author in this series, Dr Richard Hale, who has a unique ability of getting to the truth of leadership through his action learning approach – see:

http://richardhale-learninginaction.blogspot.com

Insight Coaching & Mentoring Programme

Underpinning the material within this and other workbooks in this series is the idea that coaching and mentoring are not entirely different concepts. At this stage suffice to say there is much debate about the difference between coaching and mentoring and we explore this in the next section. However, it can be seen from model below that whilst we see them as two distinct activities, there are some skills and concepts which apply equally to both coaching and mentoring.

Looking at mentoring in this way moves us beyond the question of *'Is this mentoring or coaching?'* and encourages us to be clear regarding the purpose as far as both parties in the relationship are concerned, and to be aware of the skills and behaviours which are being used to support the relationship.

Coaching and Mentoring

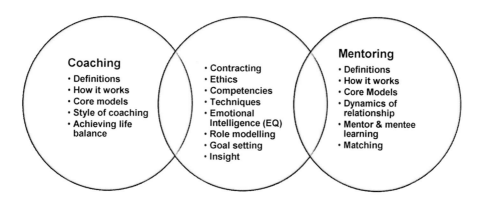

The model above suggests a number of key issues that need to be considered when seeking to understand the nature of coaching and mentoring.

In the middle circle of the model there are certain aspects which apply to both coaching and mentoring.

This includes the need in the early stages of the coaching or mentoring relationship to discuss what is often referred to as the phychological contracting stage. This is where each person agrees their role and how they plan to operate and share expectations of each other.

It is also important to consider the ethical dimension of the relationship. This includes the need to work according to a mutually acceptable ethical code, the need to be sensitive to personal values and beliefs. There are always power dynamics in any coaching or mentoring relationships and these should be considered and managed appropriately. Issues of confidentiality should be agreed as well as boundaries in terms of what might be disucssed in meetings.

In terms of competencies is it important for the coach or mentor to be aware of the key competencies required and there are certain techniques of coaching and mentoring which can be applied. These are discussed in more detail through the Insight series of workbooks.

Insight Coaching & Mentoring Programme

Both coaching and mentoring require good use of emotional intelligence, which is often referred to as EQ, in order to understand and interpret the emotions and feelings of the mentee or coachee. Understanding of emotional intelligence has advanced considerably over recent years and there are certain techinques and skills which can be developed in this field.

Coaches and mentors are often seen as role models and should recognise the importance of their own behaviours. Behaviours may be seen as an indication of personal values and beliefs and the coach or mentor is seen as a role model to the learner.

In both coaching and mentoring there is usually a place for goal setting. The coach or mentor may assist the goal setting process, whether this relates to short term goals to support the development of specific skill or longer terms goals related to career or personal development.

Depending on the context and purpose of the coaching or mentoring realtionship there may be a role in supporting the learner to consider issues of achieving a life balance. A model and tool to support discussion and consideration of this is provided in section 4 of this workbook.

Finally in the middle circle is the word 'insight'. A powerful benefit of coaching and mentoring is the way in which the learner can be supported in achieving learning insights. This might include for instance self-insight into one's abilities or behaviour in certain situations or with certain people. Insights in the context of learning are about developing wisdom and take the learning process beyond simply knowledge or skills.

In the left and right circles there are certain apsects of the coaching and mentoring role which may be quite distinctive and need to be considered in developing an understanding of either coaching or mentoring. Included here are definitions which are discussed in this workbook in some depth. Studies have also shown there are different types of coaching and approaches to mentoring which need to be considered. Whilst both coaching and mentoring are seen as learning focused relationshps we have conducted some in depth research which shows the nature of learning in the mentoring relatonship and this is shared in the article in this workbook.

Consider your own views on how coaching and mentoring are related or different and make notes on this below.

This should reflect how you currently see coaching and mentoring as activities / roles.

Insight Coaching & Mentoring Programme

2.2 – Pause for Thought – Your Role as a Coach and Mentor

How would you describe your own experience as a coach or mentor?

What have been the biggest challenges you face?

What are the aspects of coaching or mentoring you wish to develop in yourself?

Insight Coaching & Mentoring Programme

2.3 – Reflective Learning

Reflection is a key aspect of coaching and mentoring. A good coach or mentor will help the learner to reflect on their experience and to learn from it.   This is something we all do to a greater or lesser extent naturally but in a coaching or mentoring relationship the process of reflection is more deliberate. Learning from experience involves looking back at your experience and then looking forward to future activities and considering how you might do things differently as a result of your reflections. For reflection to be effective it needs to be 'critical' which means looking at your own experience, actions and emotions with a critical eye.

Reflective Exercise

To reinforce the value of reflection complete this short exercise by thinking of a real situation which you have experienced recently from which there has been some useful learning:

'What did I do?'	
'How did I feel at the time?'	
'What was the impact or effect of my actions and behaviour?'	
'What could I have done differently?'	
'What did other people think about what I did?'	
'What will I do differently?'	
'What have I learnt about myself and others and what knowledge, skills and insights have I gained?'	

Insight Coaching & Mentoring Programme

Models of Reflection

There are many 'models of reflection and as a coach or mentor it is appropriate to form a clear view regarding your own beliefs about learning and reflection. Below are some models which are provided that might be of benefit.

Kolb – Experiential Learning

Kolb D. (1984) proposed a model of learning that has become widely known and used as a basis for considering how we learn from experience. This is often referred to as the experiential learning cycle.

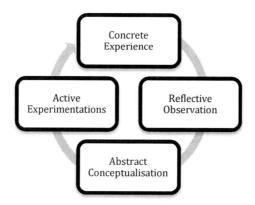

The experiential learning model suggests four learning stages and style preferences whereby 'immediate or concrete experiences' provide a basis for 'observations and reflections'. These 'observations and reflections' are distilled into 'abstract concepts' producing new implications for action that can be 'actively tested' in turn creating new experiences.

Coaching and mentoring relationships are concerned with supporting learning and it can be helpful to guide the learner through understanding the experiential model and considering how to move through the stages based on addressing real challenges they face.

Consider other learning models that may assist you in your coaching/mentoring role

Insight Coaching & Mentoring Programme

The 'What' Format of Structured Reflection

Based on Borton, T (1970) Reach, Teach and Touch. Mc Graw Hill, London and Boud D, Keogh R & Walker D (1985): Promoting reflection in learning: A model. *IN Reflection: Turing Experience into Learning* (Eds: Boud D, Keogh R & Walker D). Kogan Page, London.

The framework provides a structure for reviewing learning by looking as situations and considering the following questions and headings. A coach or mentor may help a learner to reflect on real life experiences and to consider learning which may influence future actions.

WHAT? (Returning to the situation)	SO WHAT? (Understanding the context)	NOW WHAT? (Modifying the outcomes)
• What is the purpose of returning to this situation? • What exactly occurred (in your own words)? • What did you see and do? • What was your reaction? • What did other people do, e.g. colleague, client? • What do you see as the key aspects of this situation?	• What were your feelings at the time? • What are your feelings now? Are they different, if so, why? • What 'good' emerged from the situation, e.g. self and others? • What troubles you about this situation? • What were your experiences in comparison to your colleagues or clients, etc? • What are the main reasons for feeling differently from other people who might be involved in this situation?	• What are the implications for you and your colleagues or clients etc? • What needs to happen to alter/improve the situation? • What are you going to do about the situation? • What might happen if you decide not to alter anything? • What might you do differently if faced with a similar situation again? • What information do you need in order to face a similar future situation? • What are the best ways of getting further information about the situation should it arise again?

Insight Coaching & Mentoring Programme

Reflection In and On Action (Schon 1992)

Schon advocates two types of reflection. The reflective practitioner is characterised by various qualities and abilities; is able to self-evaluate particularly in these two ways:

> **Reflection-in-action** – the practitioner is able to reflect on a situation whilst performing it. In other words, is able to change the direction of the situation accordingly.

> **Reflection-on-action** – the practitioner looks back and critically analyses the situation, with a view to doing things differently, next time a similar or the same situation arises.

	Make notes below giving an example of where you have been able to learn in both these ways. Use this structure to encourage your mentee to learn in both reflective ways.
Reflection-in-action	
Reflection-on-action	

Insight Coaching & Mentoring Programme

Moon, Reflection Techniques

J. Moon (1999) Reflection in Learning and Professional Development: Theory & Practice, Kogan Page, London proposes the following techniques for encouraging reflection:

Writing from different perspectives: You write about your experience of an exercise/event in the third person to help promote a different viewpoint in looking at a problem.

Unsent letter: Writing the experience in the form of an honest open letter to someone. The letter is then kept in the journal.

Reflection on a book or reading assignment: Using the journal to keep a running commentary on reading and writing tasks - a good way of encouraging feelings about a piece of literature.

A critical friend: Assigning partners over a set period of time for the purpose of comparing and criticising experiences and approaches. I do not like the word criticising can we change it to reviewing

Describing the process of solving problems: Taking a structured approach to identifying a sequence of stages in the process of problem-solving.

Focussing on past experience that has relevance for current learning: Drawing parallels with different experiences may provide a new outlook and promote a more imaginative approach.

Lists: Writing lists can generate lots of ideas 'What am I good at?', 'Things I could change to encourage me to read more'.

Stepping stones: Starting with a topic/experience in mind, list in chronological order, your memories of this 'event'. By promoting memory recall, this often brings about unexpected experiences.

Insight Coaching & Mentoring Programme

3 – Coaching and Mentoring: What's the Difference?

3.1 – Defining Mentoring

There is much debate about the difference between coaching and mentoring and at times it might be seen that this serves mainly to satisfy the intellectual curiosity of the specialists working in this area. However, it is worth spending a little time looking at some of the definitions of both terms and it is reasonable to expect that if you are working as a coach or a mentor, you should be able to define how you see these respective roles.

First let's look at some definitions of mentoring:

Mentoring is… 'Off-line help by one person to another in making significant transitions in knowledge, work or thinking.'
The European Mentoring Centre quoted in Clutterbuck, D., *Learning Alliances*, CIPD, 1998.

'A protected relationship, in which experimentation, exchange and learning can occur, and skills, knowledge and insight can be developed.'
Mumford, A., *How Managers Can Develop Managers*, Gower, Aldershot, 1993, p.103.

A Mentor is… 'an experienced individual, outside of the reporting relationship, who through regular meetings and discussion, takes a personal interest in guiding and supporting the development of a person in progressing beyond his or her immediate role.'
Hale, R., *Powering Up Performance Management*, Gower, 2000.

'… one-to-one process of helping individuals to learn and develop' and they noted that it 'takes a longer-term perspective which focuses on the person's career and their development. It is distinguished from coaching which has a more immediate performance-based focus.'
Tabbron, A., Macaulay, S. and Cook, S., 'Making Mentoring Work', *Training for Quality*, 5, No 1, 1997, pp. 6-9.p.6.

'…that person who achieves a one-to-one developmental relationship with a learner and one whom the learner identifies as having enabled personal growth to take place.'
Bennetts, C., *Mentors, Mirrors, and Reflective Practitioners; An Inquiry into Informal Mentor/Learner Relationships*, The University of Sheffield, 1994.

What are the key themes emerging from these definitions of mentoring?

Insight Coaching & Mentoring Programme

Now consider the definitions below:

'Mentorship is defined as an intense work relationship between senior (mentor) and junior (protégé) organizational members. The mentor has experience and power in the organization and personally advises, counsels, coaches, and promotes the career development of the protégé.'
Chao, G.T., Walz, P.M. and Gardener, P.D., 'Formal and Informal Mentorships: A Comparison on Mentoring Functions and Contrast With Nonmentored Counterparts', *Personnel Psychology,* 45, 1992, *p.624.*

'Traditionally mentors are defined as individuals with advanced experience and knowledge who are committed to providing upward mobility and support to their protégés" careers.'
Ragins, B.R., 'Diversified Mentoring Relationships in Organisations: A Power Perspective', *Academy of Management Review,* 22, No 2, 1997, p.484.

'Today, with a broader and more immediately available range of potential mentors, the term mentor seems to indicate primarily a sponsor, one who argues another's case to senior management.'
Clawson, J.G., 'Is Mentoring Necessary?', *Training & Development Journal,* April, 1985, p.36.

'Mentoring in organizations has been defined as a developmental relationship between an individual (*protégé*) and a more senior and influential manager or professional (*mentor*).'
Dreher, G.F. and Cox, T.H., 'Race, Gender, and Opportunity: A Study of Compensation Attainment and the Establishment of Mentoring Relationships', *Journal of Applied Psychology,* 81, No 3, 1996, p.298.

'A relationship between a younger adult and an older, more experienced adult that helps the individual learn to navigate in the world of work.'
Kram, K.E., *Mentoring at Work: Developmental Relationships in Organisational Life,* Scott Foresman, Glenview, IL, 1985 p.2.

How do these definitions compare with those shown in the first list?

What are the significant differences?

Insight Coaching & Mentoring Programme

The first list shows definitions taken from European authors and the second list is taken from the USA. It can be seen that there are some subtle differences in how mentoring is defined. The European definitions tend to focus more on a relationship which is outside of the 'line' relationship, and which is primarily focused on the development of the mentee. The American definitions tend to focus on the concept of the 'protégé' and progression for upward career moves. Maybe this is a cultural difference related to the theme of the American Dream and the 'self made man'. This is not to say that in European mentoring there is no consideration of upward mobility, it is just that it seems to be more overt in American definitions. A critical finding in our own research was that on occasions organisations will establish mentoring schemes without really thinking through what the purpose is. This is when it is likely to fail; it is critical to be clear as to the purpose of setting up mentoring. It is also important to differentiate between deliberate structured mentoring as seen in many organisational schemes and informal mentoring relationships which often evolve informally and which can be very powerful.

Summarise your own experience of either being mentored or mentoring others.

How would you describe the purpose of mentoring?

To what extent was this purpose overtly discussed between mentor and mentee?

Insight Coaching & Mentoring Programme

3.2 – The Context and Stages of Mentoring

There is much evidence of mentoring in the voluntary and public sector and here mentoring is often intended to provide pastoral and psycho-social support. This can be seen for instance with initiatives announced by the government in the UK in 2000 to provide mentoring for young people. Also there are examples of initiatives within voluntary sector organisations such as those in the Australian Red Cross and the Salvation Army reported by MacGregor, (1999).

Many reports concern mentoring for managers (Conway, 1996; Engstrom, 1999; Mumford, 1995; Kram and Hall, 1991). This category can be seen to overlap in some cases with that of graduate mentoring as invariably those in organisational graduate development schemes are being developed for managerial roles. However there has been an increasing interest in how the lessons learned in the various fields of mentoring can be applied in the managerial context.

Much has been written both in North America and Europe concerning graduate mentoring which is often associated with mentoring of those identified as having high potential. Several of the schemes reported by the IDS (1996) such as those as Bass, British Aerospace, Pilkington, Royal Ordinance and Prudential were targeted specifically at graduates. The Scottish Hydro-Electric Developer scheme reported by Hale (1999) also falls into this category.

With the development of the interest in continuing professional development throughout the 1990s there have been attempts to formalise the role of mentoring in this arena. This has been seen for instance with the efforts of the Chartered Institute of Personnel and Development in its former existence as the Institute of Personnel Management. Similarly mentoring has attracted attention in the field of professional development in the health sector (Morton-Cooper and Palmer, 1993). In some contexts mentoring is seen as a means of aiding the professional development of new 'mentees' coming into the profession. Here the role may be seen as more instrumental, involving an active part in aiding the development of skills as well as an enabling role.

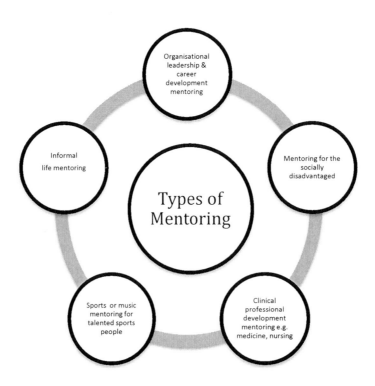

Insight Coaching & Mentoring Programme

Mentoring Approaches

Brockbank and McGill define mentoring within the context of its purpose, process and learning outcomes. They suggest there are different approaches to mentoring including Functionalist, Engagement and Evolutionary.

1 - Functionalist Approach

A functionalist approach is said to be one which is focused on efficiency, performance and maintaining prevailing norms and values. It is argued that this need to maintain the status quo tends to result in a suppressing of open debate and opportunities to challenge existing norms. Moreover it is argued that this approach tends to reinforce existing power relations within an organization or society and helps to recreate and maintain social inequalities. Essentially the functionalist approach is seen as one which is hierarchical and directive with emphasis placed on the giving of advice and the transmission of knowledge. An example of a functionalist mentor is one who is older and/or more powerful, one who serves as a guide and teacher and one who is engaged with the grooming of the mentee for career and workplace goals. Traditional mentoring of apprentices and those mentoring programmes primarily concerned with meeting organisational objectives can be said to be functionalist in nature.

2 - Engagement Approach

Unlike the functionalist approach an engagement approach can be said to be one which is non-directive and broadly humanist in nature. Nevertheless an engagement approach is regarded by some theorists as one which serves to maintain the existing power relations in organisations and society and one which may be used as a form of surveillance, regulation and social control (Colley 2003). Examples of an engagement approach include those interventions aimed at disaffection and social exclusion and the business/education partnerships which serve to groom mentees in preparation for entry into the labour market. Within a corporate environment an engagement approach can be seen as a key strategy which can be used to help facilitate the development of human resources in pursuance of organisational objectives. An example of a corporate engagement approach includes those organisations engaged in restructuring programmes who utilise the services of mentors and coaches to help assimilate employees into these programmes and new work practices.

There has been much development in recent years in mentoring of young people, particularly with a focus on young people who may be disaffected, vulnerable or socially excluded. Some key findings can be seen in the studies summarised below.

Mentoring for Vulnerable Young People: Kate Philip, Janet Shucksmith and Caroline King, 2004, Joseph Rowntree Foundation

This study looked at the impact of mentoring on young people in three settings: a housing project and an education project where paid keyworkers acted as mentors and a befriending scheme where volunteers acted as mentors. The study found:

- The friendly nature of the relationship and the 'ability to have a laugh' with a mentor distinguished these from other kinds of relationship.
- Mentoring within all the projects offered a form of 'professional' friendship. This demanded delicate negotiation between young people and mentors of the boundaries of what they would discuss, levels of confidentiality, and the time devoted by both parties.

- Most young people found the experience a positive one, contributing to their confidence, skills and development in a number of ways. Mentors also expressed satisfaction, seeing it as giving them the chance to work with rather than on young people.
- Young people particularly valued mentors who shared and were willing to discuss similar backgrounds and experiences. They felt these relationships differed from those they had with other professionals and adults. A number had been inspired to become mentors or to work with young people themselves.
- A key benefit of a good mentoring relationship was in helping young people to come to terms with difficult family relationships.

For some participants their relationship with their mentor created a safe space in which to tell their story and to rehearse what they would like to do with their lives. For many this helped them to develop ways of dealing with difficult situations and surviving in hostile environments. Key to this process was the opportunity to negotiate with the mentor, typically described as more likely to happen when 'you could have a laugh' with the mentor.

Continuity of contact was important: managing this demanded careful planning by mentors and the agency. Mentoring programmes (especially those which are tied to employment training) often neglect the process of ending the relationship. However, this could undermine the immediate benefits perceived by young people and reinforce feelings of rejection. This issue was highly significant for these young people.

Mentoring disaffected young people: an evaluation of 'Mentoring Plus', 2004: Michael Shiner, Tara Young, Tim Newburn and Sylvie Groben. , Joseph Rowntree Foundation

This is an evaluation of ten mentoring programmes designed to work with hard-to-reach teenagers. Mentoring has emerged as the latest in a long line of interventions aimed at reducing youth disaffection. Although mentoring has become a very popular response to youth disaffection there is little evidence as to its effectiveness. The key findings were:

Mentoring disaffected young people was found to be a delicate, cyclical and reactive process. Many relationships did not progress beyond basic 'mundane' social interaction on to specific problem-focused or goal-oriented activity.

Evidence of impact was most marked in relation to engagement in education, training and work. Participation in the programme was associated with a heightened rate of engagement in these areas.

There was no clear evidence of the programme having an impact in relation to offending, family relationships, substance use and self-esteem.

The programme appeared to be particularly successful in engaging those young people who were at most risk of social exclusion, including significant numbers of Black African/Caribbean young people.

This study found mentoring to be a delicate process based largely on 'ordinary' social interaction which often has little obvious connection with responding to challenging behaviour or the causes or consequences of social exclusion. Typically it is cyclical and reactive. The research team identified three potential cycles:

- the basic cycle: contact-meeting-doing;
- the problem-solving cycle: contact-meeting-doing-fire-fighting;
- the action-oriented cycle: contact-meeting-doing-fire-fighting-action.

Insight Coaching & Mentoring Programme

The activities in the basic cycle were generally fairly mundane - having tea/coffee, playing pool, shopping, bowling, or perhaps going to the cinema - and many relationships did not progress much beyond this. Proactive planning and action were relatively rare. Where relationships did progress beyond the basic cycle, they often did so in response to a problem or crisis (e.g. homelessness, family breakdown, specific forms of offending, substance misuse, violent behaviour). Some relationships did progress beyond the reactive fire-fighting stage to become genuinely action-oriented and closer to what often appears to be the typical conception of ideal mentoring. Where relationships progressed, they tended to do so fairly late on, once trust had developed and key issues were identified.

Interventions with disaffected young people are inherently difficult to implement and these difficulties are exacerbated by insecure funding, fixed-term employment for project workers and high staff turnover.

3 - Evolutionary Approach

An evolutionary approach is one that is essentially humanistic and person-centered in nature. Here the mentee's thoughts, ideas and experiences are respected and he/she is encouraged to assume ownership of his/her life and goals. It is argued that this approach is essentially transformative and that the open and reflective dialogue which is a hallmark of this approach leads to an examination of existing power structures and social norms which may have served to inhibit the mentees learning and personal development. It is further argued that the potential for transformation and empowerment which this approach engenders leads to benefits for both mentee and the organisation to which they are aligned. Evolutionary mentoring often takes place as part of a private arrangement between mentee and mentor outside of the work environment.

Evolutionary mentoring is defined as *'an agreed activity between mentor and client, where goals are generated by and for the client, the process is person-centered and the learning outcome is transformation.'* Brockbank & McGill (2006:75).

Mentoring Developmental Stages

The mentoring relationship can be seen as dynamic and continually evolving. Some authors have tried to identify discrete phases and stages of development in the relationship. It is argued that if successful mentoring relationships are to be achieved, it is essential that mentors develop an understanding of the various stages, the work that is required at each stage and how each stage complements and supports the mentoring process as a whole.

Zachary (2000) has drawn up four phases which typify the mentoring relationship. Zachary also highlights a recurring theme in this module, the importance of refection arguing that it is an integral part of the process and must accompany each of the mentoring phases, starting during the preparing phase and continuing until closure is reached. In this model, the focus is not so much on time frames but on behaviours.

Preparing Phase

The first phase of the mentoring relationship is the preparing phase. She argues that this phase is essentially a process of discovery and will involve an evaluation of the prospective partnership together with the establishment of a framework on which to deliver the mentoring. Issues such as personal motivation, roles and expectations will all be considered at this phase. Mentors will also use this phase to assess their current mentoring skills in order to identify areas for further development and learning.

Insight Coaching & Mentoring Programme

Negotiating Phase

The second phase of this model is the negotiating phase. This is the "detail phase" and a time when agreement is reached on the goals, content and process of the mentoring relationship. It is argued that this phase has more to do with developing a mutual understanding about assumptions, expectations, goals and needs than drawing up a formal written agreement. This phase should be used to articulate and clarify issues on accountability, confidentiality and boundaries. This phase should also be used to get clear on more practical issues such as the scheduling and frequency of meetings, shared and individual responsibilities, the criteria which will be used to measure success and how and when the relationship will be brought to closure.

Enabling Phase

At this stage the mentor is focused on nurturing the mentee's growth by creating open and affirming learning conditions and ensuring that the mentee receives timely and constructive feedback. Both the mentor and mentee are equally engaged in monitoring the process and the progress made in achieving the mentee's goals. The enabling phase as a process of path building and argues that even when the process and goals of the relationship are well defined and articulated, every mentoring relationship is unique and must find its own path. This phase is very much the implementation phase of the relationship and will necessarily take a longer period of time than the other three phases. It is also a complex phase and Zachary argues that the mentoring partners are vulnerable to a myriad of obstacles which can lead to the derailment of the relationship. As such there will be a need to work on developing and maintaining a level of trust and open and clear channels of communication between the partners.

Coming to Closure

The fourth and final phase of the mentoring relationship is the closure phase. This is an evolutionary process which has a beginning (the inclusion of closure protocols when drawing up the mentoring agreement) a middle (anticipating and addressing obstacles as they arise) and an end (ensuring positive learning outcomes). These three components are seen as essential for a satisfactory closure. Mentors and mentees who encounter obstacles along the way may find it useful to work their way back through the various phases, as this will enable them to evaluate and recharge a stalled relationship. There is also a need here to be sensitive to the signals indicating the need for closure as this too will help to ensure a timely and positive ending. The time for closure may occur for example, when goals are attained or in cases where a relationship is counterproductive or dysfunctional.

Whatever the determining factor, closure will involve a process of evaluation as well as acknowledgment and celebration of any achievements. Mentors also need to be aware of the fact that not all achievements will necessarily be tangible ones or ones which can easily be measured. There may well be other equally important intangible or difficult to measure achievements for example in the gaining of new attitudes and perspectives or the development of social skills, which may be critical to the mentee's overall future development. Moreover closure should be seen not only as an opportunity to evaluate learning but how that leaning can be applied to future relationships and situations.

Insight Coaching & Mentoring Programme

Consider a mentoring relationship where you have been the mentor or the mentee. Consider the phases that the relationship passed through and how they relate to the model described above.

Insight Coaching & Mentoring Programme

3.3 – Defining Coaching

Consider some definitions of coaching below:

Coaching is unlocking a person's potential to maximise their own performance. It is helping them to learn rather than teaching them.'
Whitmore, J., (1996*). Coaching for Performance*, Nicholas Brearley, London.

'Coaching is conceived as a more structured learning process aimed at explicit professional development in an agreed area(s) of performance.'
Pennington, R.C., (2004) *Developing Leaders for Today and The Future*. Sheffield: Higher Education Staff Development Agency.

'Coaching is a process that enables learning and development to occur and thus performance to improve. To be a successful coach requires a knowledge and understanding of the process as well as a variety of styles, skills and techniques that are appropriate to the context in which the coaching takes place.'
Parsloe, E., (1996). *The Manager as Coach and Mentor*, IPD, London.

'Coaching is a management skill and is distinct from mentoring, training and counselling. Each has a role in the workplace and it is useful to establish how they may be appropriately applied.'
Hill. P., (2000) *Concepts of Coaching: a guide for managers.*

'Coaching is unlocking a person's potential to maximise their own performance. It is helping them to learn rather than teaching them.'
Whitmore, J., (1996) *Coaching for Performance*, Nicholas Brearly, London

'Coaching is conceived as a more structured learning process aimed at explicit professional development in an agreed area(s) of performance.'
Pennington, R.C., (2004) *Developing Leaders for Today and The Future*. Sheffield: Higher Education Staff Development Agency.

Coaching can be defined in various ways. It has, for example, been described as: "unlocking a person's potential to maximise their own performance. It is "helping them to learn rather than teaching them," (Gallwey, 1975); "a process that enables learning and development to occur and thus performance to improve," (Parsloe, 1999); a flexible process "whereby an individual, through direct discussion and guided activity, helps a colleague to learn to solve a problem or to do a task better than would be otherwise the case," (Megginson and Baydell,1979); and concerning itself "with amplifying the individual's own knowledge and thought processes. It is about creating a supportive environment in which to challenge and develop critical thinking skills." (Guest, D. 1999)
Institute of Leadership and Management 2011.

'For me coaching means supporting my clients to realize their true potential and therefore the unique potential that is their right.'
Sue Knight, international NLP coach and trainer 2011 NLP at Work

'Coaching will strengthen character, develop an influential skill set. Coaching is based on sincere and honest dialogue, challenging perceptions, attitudes and behaviour in a safe and secure environment. Coaching is multifaceted, affording the opportunity to evaluate and appraise the value of personal attributes.'   This is an expressive view of the authors as mentioned in the Insight cycle. of coaching and mentoring.

Insight Coaching & Mentoring Programme

> **What are the key themes emerging from these definitions of coaching?**
>
>
>

How do we define other forms of coaching?

Coaching can be used for various purposes and there are different types and models of coaching being used in all walks of life, ranging from the business to the public and charitable sectors. Below we provide some of the categories of coaching along with some definitions. This is not an exhaustive list and you will see that there are potentially some areas of overlap. However this may help you to consider your own roles as a coach and the purpose or sort of coaching you are providing, depending on the needs of your client.

- **Performance coaching:** This is primarily designed to enhance an individual's performance within their current role at work, or to improve their capabilities and productivity at work. In general, performance coaching derives its theoretical foundations and models from business and sports psychology as well as general psychological theory.

- **Skills Coaching:** This type of coaching concentrates on the basic skills a person needs to perform in their role. Skills' coaching provides a flexible, adaptive approach to skills development and delivers it at the time when it is most needed. Coaching programmes are tailored specifically to the individual and are generally focused on achieving a number of skill development objectives that are linked to the needs of the organisation. Some organisations will implement a mentoring skills programme to achieve the same objective as the skills coaching.

Insight Coaching & Mentoring Programme

- **Career Coaching:** A career coach is a person that has been trained in helping other people develop their career goals. Even if you are unsure of your career goals, a career coach will work closely with you in order to help you determine where you would like your career to go and to develop a plan for achieving those goals. We have developed an approach to career coaching which encourages the coachee to review their career to date as a journey. By reflecting back on the journey, your clients will be able to develop and plan a way forward. This process will equip them to identify the next steps needed. You can then assist them to formulate Action Learning Questions to help them move towards their career goals.

- **Personal or Life coaching:** This form of coaching provides support to individuals wishing to make some form of significant change within their lives. Coaches help individuals to explore what they want in life and how they might achieve their aspirations and fulfil their needs. Personal or life coaching generally takes the individual's agenda as its start point.

- **Business Coaching:** Business coaching is conducted within the constraints placed on the individual or group by the organisational context. It may relate to or cross over with career coaching and it usually involves providing support in tackling specific business challenges, which may be technical, behavioural or team related.

- **Executive Coaching:** An executive coach is a specialised type of career coach that focuses on helping a senior person within an organisation by providing a trusted and confidential relationship. An executive coach often helps with challenges such as managing corporate politics, personal challenges and career objectives. In some cases the aim is to achieve career progression, in others it may be about using coaching to help work out next career steps or moves. Equally, executive coaching may be problem-centred and focus on how to address major challenges in the organisation.

- **Team Facilitation Coaching:** Coaching a team in a facilitation role is particularly valuable when a team is facing a significant challenge, or where it may be facing difficulty in terms of intra-team relations. If you think of the role of a sports coach working with a team, the coach will add particular value when there is a major competition challenge. Equally, a good sports team coach will understand individual team personalities and team dynamics and will be able to manage these effectively.

- **Peer Coaching and Action Learning:** This is a dynamic form of coaching that builds on the psychological fact that people often pay more attention to the feedback, guidance and behaviour of their peers than they do to those perceived as in authority positions. Peer coaching can be very powerful; however it needs to be set up in a sensitive way so that there is acceptance by all parties that it is possible to learn with and from each other. This links in many ways to the principles of Action Learning where people come together as peers in a 'learning set', and support each other in tackling work-based problems using a questions-based approach. On occasion peers may be able to provide specific technical advice about solving problems or development of certain skills; however the power of the Action Learning approach lies more in the idea of asking insightful and thought-provoking questions of each other.

- **NLP Coaching:** This is a dynamic and effective form of coaching and by using Neuro-Linguistic Programming within the coaching arena you can bring about lasting change to both personal and business issues. The focus is based on understanding, recognising and making changes to how we conduct ourselves. NLP is an effective tool for the client to examine thoughts, beliefs and values. NLP teaches us the tools and techniques to become the person we really want to be. NLP coaching is about personal

Insight Coaching & Mentoring Programme

transformation and helping you achieve more balance in every aspect of your life. We provide more information specifically on the application of NLP in module 3 of the Insight series.

Summarise your own experience of either being coached or coaching others.

How would you describe the purpose of coaching? What category of coaching based on the above list is most relevant to you? Why?

Insight Coaching & Mentoring Programme

3.4 – Comparing Coaching and Mentoring

Now that we have considered some of the definitions, purposes and categories of coaching and mentoring, we realise there are some distinctive aspects of each but there are also some common skills and processes which are required in order to be effective as a coach or a mentor. In the corporate context some of the differences have been summarised by one author below.

Comparing Coaching and Mentoring	
Source Clutterbuck, D., *Learning Alliances, 1998*	
Coaching	**Mentoring**
Concerned with task	Concerned with implications beyond task
Focuses on skills and performance	Focuses on capacity and potential
Primarily a line manager role	Works best outside the line management relationship
Agenda set by or with the coach	Agenda set by learner
Feedback **to** the learner	Emphasises feedback and reflection **by** the learner
Addresses a short term need	Usually a longer relationship
Feedback and discussion is primarily explicit.	Feedback and discussion about implicit and intuitive issues and behaviours.

Insight Coaching & Mentoring Programme

Another useful model which helps explain where mentoring and coaching fits as developmental relationships is shown below. Here you can see that towards the left of the continuum, the focus is more on inner issues determined by the person seeking to develop. Towards the right the focus is more on imparting knowledge or skills which might be pre-determined, and the process tends to be delivered by one person to another. It can be seen that coaching and mentoring are not actually that far apart and it is understandable that on occasions the roles may overlap.

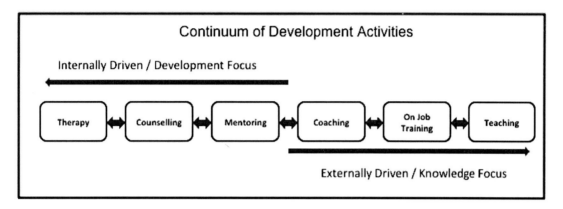

It is important to differentiate coaching and mentoring from counselling and therapy. The British Association of Counselling and Psychotherapy says:

Counselling takes place when a counsellor sees a client in a private and confidential setting to explore a difficulty the client is having, distress they may be experiencing or perhaps their dissatisfaction with life, or loss of a sense of direction and purpose. It is always at the request of the client as no-one can properly be 'sent' for counselling.

Therapy tends to be associated with an objective of healing and is often related to diagnosed mental or physical problems or illnesses. The subjects of counselling and therapy are out of the scope of our work and publication as we are focused specifically on the development of coaching and mentoring awareness and capability.

It is however critically important for any coach or mentor to know their capabilities and limitations and if you find the person you are working with is experiencing difficulty, you may need to encourage them to seriously consider getting professional support from a therapist. In our personal coaching and mentoring practices we often work with clients who either receive counselling or psychotherapy.

When taking on the role of coach or mentor it is important to carefully consider your own capabilities and to review your own performance with a view to undertaking CPD (continuous professional development), and whilst some people are often considered to have a natural coaching or mentoring ability or inclination, there are certain skills which you should seek to consciously develop. We provide more information specifically on the application of coaching and mentoring capabilities in module 2 of the Insight series.

Insight Coaching & Mentoring Programme

Continuous Professional Development Planner

Consider and summarise your own CPD below. Remember to include both professional and personal learning and development needs.

What would you like to achieve in the next 12 month period?

How would you like to develop yourself?

What expertise or skill will you need for the future?

Are there any particular problems you would like to solve?

Insight Coaching & Mentoring Programme

3.5 – Benefits of Mentoring

Benefits for the Mentee

The evidence from our research suggests the real power of mentoring is in the development of insights and we explore this in more detail in later Modules during the programme. Insights begin more with the individual, emerge for the individual, are assisted by the effective mentor and are more personal. The development of insights is less easily planned; whether or not they emerge will depend on the real-life circumstances and experiences of the mentee and the extent to which the mentor can assist the mentee in making the connection between an experience and him or herself. Insights are often associated with wisdom. Here is how Alan Mumford distinguishes between knowledge, skills and insights in the process of learning:

'Knowledge is the acquisition of data or information. Sometimes it is not new knowledge but confirmation of past information. Skills are the means used to carry out managerial work effectively. The most obvious examples include making decisions, running meetings and negotiating. Insight or perceptiveness – some people would call it developing wisdom. You can acquire knowledge and skills, but lack the extra dimension provided through insight. Insight is often expressed as conclusions; it helps you generalise from particular experiences.'

MUMFORD, A. , *How Managers Can Develop Managers,* Gower, 1993

Examples of insights might be:

- Realising how to influence a particular person more effectively based on understanding their personality style.
- Realising how one's own preferred style of leadership may need to be adapted in certain circumstances.
- Realising the real motives behind someone else's behavior.
- Realising why you feel particular emotions in certain situations.

Consider when you last achieved an insight. Describe it starting with the following words:

'I realised...

Now consider how you achieved the insight. How did you connect knowledge with a real situation? Did another person help you achieve the insight and if so, how?

Insight Coaching & Mentoring Programme

Mentoring can also help in the development of the mentee in a number of other ways:

- It can help unblock some of the barriers which may be preventing an individual from making changes in the way they operate. For instance, supporting the development of self-belief may help an individual into action orientation and encourage them to take risks in a calculated way - which actually supports their development.
- Mentoring can help ensure skills development is transferred to the job and is sustainable.
- Mentoring can help the development of confidence on the part of the mentee and this may result in more sustained changes than, say, increased confidence achieved through a short training course alone, perhaps.
- Mentoring provides a powerful vehicle for discussing inter-personal relationships including the mentee's relationship with his or her line manager.

Benefits for the Mentor

Often when mentoring initiatives are set up in an organisation, the main focus is placed on the development of the mentee in the relationship. However it is clear that there are potential benefits for the mentor, and these are more likely to be realised if they are considered at the outset. It sounds like an obvious question to ask a mentor: *'What are you looking for from the relationship?'*, but it is often forgotten and learning opportunities may be wasted. Here are some of the benefits that mentors have reported.

- Reflection on their own development needs, prompted by encouraging the mentee to address the same issue
- Refreshment of their own skills through having to guide the mentee
- Appreciation of the role of the mentee and his or her part of the business
- Development of their own style of management or leadership through experimentation in the role of mentor
- Insight into how they were perceived by others in the business
- Satisfaction in being able to pass on wisdom to younger members of the organisation.

Benefits for the Organisation

Many organisations have realised the benefits of setting up mentoring initiatives and these can be summarised as follows:

- Mentoring supports challenging upwards, as the mentee gains confidence to question how things are done within the organisation
- Mentees may feel more comfortable with approaching senior managers and it can encourage upward communication
- It provides access to careers advice and a realisation of the importance of managing one's own career in a proactive way
- It can help with developing an appreciation of the company culture
- It can help improve retention as mentees decide to take a long term view and stay with the organisation. Note also though that in some cases if the organisation fails to meet raised expectations it can lead to them leaving. Equally they may leave if they come to realise there is not a good fit between themselves and the organisation.

Insight Coaching & Mentoring Programme

Consider an organisation you have either worked in or with, or that you know of, which has set up a structured approach to mentoring.

Try to identify what the purpose was in setting up mentoring and consider the benefits that were achieved at an organisational level from doing so. Make notes below.

If you do not have access to such organisations you might like to read the article in this Module entitled 'To Match or Mis-Match?' The Dynamics of Mentoring as a Route to Personal and Organisational Learning'. This provides some case examples and you can make notes of organisational benefits below.

Insight Coaching & Mentoring Programme

3.6 – Benefits of Coaching

Coaching is being used in a large number of business organisations. Its accepted practice is growing fast and research to date indicates overwhelming evidence in support of coaching. Benefits are seen both by the individuals receiving the coaching and by the organisation.

In particular, benefits are seen in financial performance, retention and development of executives and in communications within organisations. A report from the Chartered Institute of Personnel and Development also provides a list of benefits for the individual and for the organisation, which it states can be used by HR to build a case for using coaching in an organisation.

Benefits for the Individual

- Improved problem solving
- Improve managerial and interpersonal skills
- Have better relationships with colleagues
- Learn how to identify and act on development needs
- Have greater confidence
- Become more effective and assertive in dealing with people
- Have a positive impact on performance
- Have greater self-awareness and gain new perspectives
- Acquire new skills and abilities
- Develop greater adaptability to change
- Improve work–life balance
- Reduce stress levels

Benefits for the Organisation

- Improves productivity, quality, customer service and shareholder value
- Can gain increased employee commitment and satisfaction, which can lead to improved retention
- Demonstrates to employees that an organisation is committed to developing its staff and helping them improve their skills
- Supports employees who've been promoted to cope with new responsibilities
- Helps employees to sort out personal issues that might otherwise affect performance at work
- Gains a satisfactory process for self-development
- Supports other training and development initiatives e.g. reduce 'leakage' from training courses

In conclusion the benefits of coaching as a development tool provide a valuable structured framework to implement both business and personal growth. Professional coaching brings complex issues to the forefront of the coaching agenda presenting a dynamic perspective and understanding of cultural receptiveness.

Insight Coaching & Mentoring Programme

We have included some brief case examples below summarizing the use of coaching and mentoring within different industries and sectors. The examples highlight and bring to life the skill set of coaching and mentoring which are being utilised to achieve personal and professional objectives. In case study 4 the authors give a personal account of how their peer to peer programme has transformed people's lives within the health sector.

Case example 1 - Hospitality Industry
The Marriott Marquis Hotel in Atlanta demonstrated impressive results after a two year coaching programme. Improvements were seen in customer satisfaction and staff retention, and unity across the diverse workforce was noted.

Case example 2 - Health Services
Fairview Health Services in Minnesota used a coaching programme to improve employee satisfaction. They found that coaching improves employee effectiveness and engagement at work. A particular success has been the retention of all 28 of the High- Potential leaders, three years after they received coaching. During September 2003, a report was issued by Compass Point, detailing many benefits of coaching for executive directors of non-profit organisations. This year-long project provided coaching to 24 executive directors. It concluded that coaching has a profound impact on them and the organisations they lead.

Case example 3 Executive Coaching
The executive directors saw benefits including improved leadership and management skills, increased confidence and improved delegation and communication skills. Coaching helped them in both their professional and personal development and helped them to cope with fast-paced change and the associated challenges. The organisations saw many benefits, including increased financial stability. Coaching was regarded as an inexpensive, high impact way to develop the leadership skills of executive directors.

Case example 4 The Mental Health Sector; Peer coaching & mentoring
HCMA (Harmony Coaching & Mentoring Avenues) developed and pioneered a highly effective peer to peer coaching & mentoring programme delivered to Mind Network, Guideposts Trust, Viewpoint and Dens in Hertfordshire. The course was written and delivered by HCMA, accredited by the Institute of Leadership and Management, and students opted for either the Endorsed or Development Award, depending on their level of experience. Subjects included: Goal setting; Motivation; Managing the relationship and well-formed outcomes.

The training was delivered to a mixture of staff, volunteers and clients. On completion of the training the clients were given the opportunity to become volunteer coaches and mentors and this progression plan really helped individuals to move on to next step in making a huge change in how they perceived themselves – In Hertfordshire there is a pool of mentors who coach others to make positive changes in their lives and overcome some of the issues around their mental health. Supervision formed part of the initiative and the outcomes from the training have literally changed people's lives. It was a very personal experience and people who suffered with low self esteem gained new insights into their personal and behavioural problems and made incredible progress.

"The Mentoring & Coaching came at just the right time for our organisation – the courses, have helped staff, volunteers and clients to support each other at a more constructive level than previously, and has helped some individuals' confidence enormously. I particularly think that the goal setting and some of the techniques, such as looking at the different areas of your own life, fits in to our holistic approach"   Manager Guideposts Watford Hertfordshire, UK.

Insight Coaching & Mentoring Programme

Consider what other benefits coaching can bring...

Benefits for the Individual

Benefits for the Organisation

Insight Coaching & Mentoring Programme

Coaching in Business and Lifestyle Coaching

During 2002, the Chartered Management Institute (CMI) published a "Coaching at Work Survey" regarding the extent of coaching in the workplace at that time. They found that of the 280 organisations surveyed, 23% had formal coaching programmes in place and a further 44% were using coaching on an ad-hoc basis.

This survey found that an overwhelming 80% of managers believed they would benefit from more coaching in their place of work. They also found that 93% of managers believe coaching should be available to all employees regardless of seniority. During April 2004, the Chartered Institute of Personnel and Development (CIPD) issued a survey report, "Training and development 2004" which evaluated the growing trend of coaching. Of 531 CIPD member organisations that responded, 78% reported that coaching was in use, and over 90% of respondents agreed with various statements regarding the effectiveness of coaching to deliver tangible benefits and promote learning.

CIPD findings indicated that of all training forms, coaching had seen the largest percentage increase in usage in recent years, higher even than e-learning. Coaching is most often used for improving personal performance and is used mainly by managers and directors. The CIPD published a subsequent report "Coaching and buying coaching services" in June 2004. This report says that the increased use of coaching has been driven by a number of factors, including:

- ability to adapt to rapid change
- organisational downsizing - means newly promoted individuals require support
- lifelong learning needs
- costs associated with poor performance
- senior level employees needing someone to confide in
- individual responsibility for development

The report states that HR/training practitioners almost universally believe "…coaching is an effective way of promoting learning and it can have an impact on the organisation's bottom line and it is capable of delivering tangible benefits to individuals and organisations."

Reflections from People Who Have Experienced Coaching

"I have been offered a career coach by my employer and it is helping me to work through the choices I have in my career at a key stage when I need to decide whether to stay as a partner or to move on into my own business." Director, major accountancy practice

"My business coach understood the importance of relevant coaching for this business. The coaching centred on the company culture and specific challenges within our organisation. This came at a critical time where we had a high attrition rate; we now have an excellent retention rate". Director of Operations, architectural company.

"I left the career workshop looking forward to developing my career instead of fearing it. It totally changed my outlook." Senior Management Consultant, design company.

"Coaching has allowed me to manage the change process for my organisation. With coaching, change became a trouble-free experience." Project Director, international cable company

"I use coaching to seek clarity and confidence. It ensures congruence in my actions and values I aspire to for myself and the company." Managing Director, furniture retailer

Insight Coaching & Mentoring Programme

"Working with my business coach we didn't just focus on activity, we looked at what prevents it and how to eliminate the blocks."   Sales & Marketing Manager, communications company

"Business Coaching has taught me self-responsibility; I've discovered a practical theory where ownership is at the core of the teaching."   New Proprietor, automotive centre

"Business Coaching helped me to bring about huge transformations in the community.   I was able to bring about beneficial change on many levels."   Chair, community charity

Consider your own experience of having been coached and provide your own quotation below regarding the value you have gained from the experience...

Insight Coaching & Mentoring Programme

3.7 – Creating a Coaching Culture (ILM perspective)

The world of work is complex and constantly changing. Fast paced and high pressured, it places increasingly tough demands on employees throughout organisations. Consequently leaders and managers at all levels need a broad portfolio of management and leadership tools and techniques to do their job effectively. Coaching is a particularly powerful tool in the modern workplace – one that has proven to be a highly effective way of developing individual and organisational performance by unlocking capability. At its best, this key management tool can deliver considerable benefits, helping managers get the most from their teams, boosting employee engagement and developing high performing workplaces. Anecdotal evidence suggests that coaching is increasingly widespread in organisations. Yet there is little objective research to tell us for certain how organisations approach the use of coaching. What, for example, is behind the rapid growth in the use of coaching? How and why do organisations use coaching, and what can we learn from them? What criteria are used to select coaches, and how is the effectiveness of coaching measured? ILM set out to provide some definitive answers to these and other related questions. Our findings establish the extent to which organisations are embracing the coaching concept, and identify and share coaching best practice. They provide valuable insights for employers looking to maximise the effectiveness of coaching, and for coaching professionals about the market they serve and the expectations of their customers.

Most companies use coaching as a development tool:
80% of organisations surveyed had used or are using coaching. Another 9% are planning to. The more employees in the organisation, the more likely it is to use coaching. 90% of organisations with 2,001+ employees used coaching in the past five years, but this fell to 68% of those with 230–500 employees.

It is mostly middle managers and above who receive coaching:
More people should be able to benefit from coaching in organisations. At present only 52% of organisations make coaching available to all their staff. By contrast, 85% of organisations surveyed said that coaching is aimed at managers and directors, and middle management.

Organisations source more coaches internally, but use external coaches to coach senior executives:
83% of organisations surveyed source coaches internally, while 65% hire them in. External coaches are used primarily to coach senior managers. Interestingly,
there is more rigour over selecting external service providers than internal coaches. Benchmarks of quality are still needed though in an unregulated coaching industry

More support is required for internal coaches:
A greater focus on developing internal coaching capacity is needed. Most organisations recognise the value of coaching qualifications. Two-thirds (66%) offer development options for coaches such as in-house training (20%), management development programmes (11%) or one-to-one train-the-trainer support (8%). A third (34%), however, do not offer
any support or development for internal coaches.

Broad consensus on the benefits of coaching:
The benefits that are obtained are well recognised and varied. 95% of respondents saw direct benefits to the organisation, and 96% saw benefits to the individual. A broad range of specific benefits were identified including improvements in communication and interpersonal skills, leadership and management, conflict resolution, personal confidence, attitudes and motivation, management performance as well as preparation for a new role or promotion.

Insight Coaching & Mentoring Programme

Coaching is aimed at improving the individual rather than the organisation:
At its best, coaching addresses personal skills and development, as well as business and work skills. More organisations use coaching for personal development (53%) than for improving specific areas of organisational performance (26%).On an individual level, though, more organisations (95%) use coaching to focus on business and workplace skills, than personal skills (70%).

Not a remedial tool:
Many organisations still view coaching as a tool for correcting poor performance. However, good coaching is about achieving a high performance culture, not managing a low performance one, and should not be seen primarily as a remedial tool.

Better measurement of coaching's effectiveness is needed:
While most organisations (93%) measure coaching outcomes, evaluation approaches are inconsistent. Some organisations simply use internal appraisal systems (70%) or 360 degree appraisal (40%), only two-fifths undertake "specific evaluation of coaching interventions", while just under half (49%) assess against business KPIs and goals.

A coaching culture:
Organisations wishing to maximise the benefits of coaching should focus on increasing its scope and availability to create a coaching culture that permeates throughout their workforce. This means that coaching must be supported at the very top of the organisation, but not limited to senior executives, and that organisations need to devote resources to developing their internal coaching capability.

Creating a Coaching Culture, Institute of Leadership & Management, May 2011

What are the key conclusions emerging from the ILM perspective?

Insight Coaching & Mentoring Programme

4 – The Wheel of Life

The wheel of life has become a well known tool and you will find it being used in both personal and professional coaching and mentoring. We have included a model below for you to consider using.

Occasionally we may find ourselves under pressure either in the work place or in our personal lives and we are not sure why. This may be because our 'Wheel of Life' is out of balance. This exercise is designed to assess the balance in your life and will help you and your Coach to identify areas to work on.

Take some time to think about your life and where you are at in the current time. Grade your level of contentment with each life area mentioned below by indicating which number, on a scale of 1 to 10, most closely matches how satisfied you are with that area of your life. For example, if you are feeling fit and well, in that case you might like to score your Health at 6 or 7, if you are not feeling fit or healthy, then you might want to score it at 3.

Insight Wheel of Life

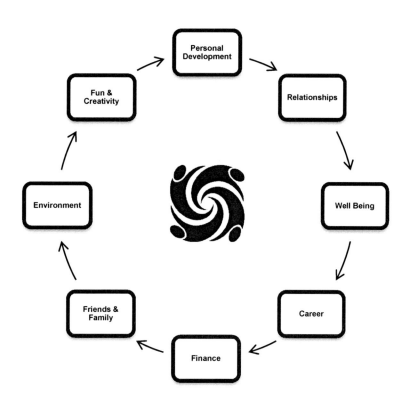

The Insight Wheel of Life as we have shown it above is adapted from the original depiction of *bhavacakra* which is a symbolic representation found in Buddist culture. It is thought in the Buddist tradition that the drawing was designed by the Buddha himself in order to help ordinary people understand the Buddhist teachings. We have adapted the concept for consideration in the context of coaching and mentoring and by working with the exercise shown below it is possible to open up a constructive process of discussion and reflection in order to support future decision making and prioritisation.

Insight Coaching & Mentoring Programme

The purpose of completing the wheel of life exercise is to gain awareness of one's internal state and once we become aware of how we manage our lives we can start to focus on any area that we may need or want to change. Take some time to reflect about each area of your life, looking at where you are now and where you want to be. Consider the areas shown below and make notes regarding the main areas that you feel you would want to make some changes.

Physical Environment

Finances

Fun and creativity

Wellbeing

Relationships

Personal Development

Career

Friends & Family

Insight Coaching & Mentoring Programme

5 – The Insight Coaching & Mentoring Cycle

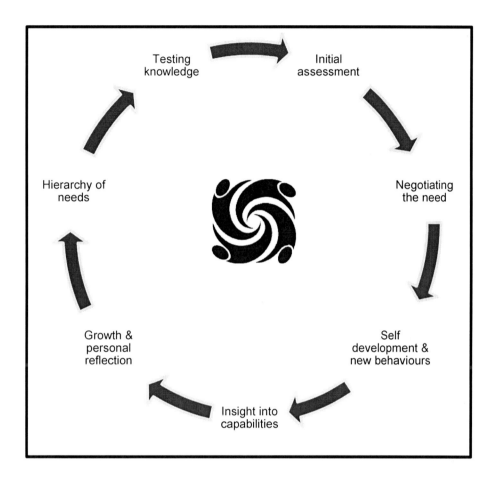

The Insight Cycle of Coaching & Mentoring gives a framework for coaching/mentoring meetings and will help the coachee/mentee to plan a way forward. The themes shown give you the opportunity to identifiy a number of key interventions that need to be well thought-out when working with clients.

The benefits of using this model will enable you to move towards being a first-class coach or mentor who will achieve strength of character, transparency and the ability to develop an influential relationship based on sincere and honest dialogue. This model will equip you to challenge perceptions, attitudes and behaviours in a safe and secure environment. Coaching and mentoring demands a skill set that is multifaceted and hands on experience is essential.

Insight Coaching & Mentoring Programme

The Insight Coaching & Mentoring Cycle

I - Initial assessment

The initial assessment will give you the opportunity to build rapport with the coachee/mentee whilst eliciting the core requirements for the coaching/mentoring intervention.

N - Negotiating the coaching/mentoring plan

Negotiating the coaching/mentoring plan is a key component of the Insight cycle, covering environment, ethical practice, preparation, time commitment and paperwork.

S -Self development and new behaviours

The self development plan or CPD (continuous personal development) will enable the coachee/mentee to identify areas for development, it will afford the coach/mentor the opportunity to suggest and discuss new behaviour techniques or new learning with the purpose of bringing about personal change.

I - Insight into own capabilities

Once the coachee/mentee engages in the first part of the Insight Cycle they will identify and discover insights into their own capabilities including reviewing both their strengths and weakness, allowing for a deeper understanding of their personal beliefs, values and goals.

G – Growth and personal reflection

The growth and personal reflection period will give the coach/mentee the time to reflect on the interventions provided with the view to monitor, review and evaluate what has worked well and what may need to be modified.

H – Hierarchy of needs

This element of the cycle will give both parties insight into the motivation and achievements to date ensuring the basic needs of the coaching/mentoring intervention have been completed before moving on to discussing more complex needs.

T – Testing new skills and knowledge

The testing stage will give the coachee/mentee time to test their new skills and knowledge within their lives, while gaining a deeper appreciation for their personal and professional achievements.

Insight Coaching & Mentoring Programme

This is just one model of coaching and mentoring as defined by the authors.

Consider your own approach and views on the process of coaching and mentoring and make notes on this and present it below.

This should reflect how you currently conceptualise coaching and mentoring and the series of interventions needed to bring about behavioural change.

Insight Coaching & Mentoring Programme

6 – Johari Window - A Model of Insight

Johari window is a cognitive psychological tool created by Joseph Luft and Harry Ingham in 1955 in the United States and it was used to help people understand their internal communication model and how they built relationships. Until recently it was principally used in therapeutic training and in self-help groups moving into the corporate sector as a heuristic exercise. Heuristic methods are understood to accelerate the process of problem solving while achieving an agreeable outcome for all concerned. The model proposes that intuitive judgment and common sense can assist people in acquiring both the knowledge and ability to overcome their own personal barriers or mental inabilities.

Charles Handy calls this concept the Johari House with four rooms. Room 1 is the part of ourselves that we see and others see. Room 2 is the aspects that others see but we are not aware of. Room 3 is the most mysterious room in that the unconscious or subconscious part of us is seen by neither ourselves nor others. Room 4 is our private space, which we know but keep from others.

This model when used in either coaching or mentoring creates deeper understanding of problems or issues affecting individuals, as it affords a framework for looking at situations from different perspectives.

	Known to self	Not known to self
Known to others	Open area	Blind area
Not known to others	Hidden area/façade	Unknown area

The model was successfully ustilised within the peer coaching and mentoring programme as mentioned in case example 4.

Insight Coaching & Mentoring Programme

Consider the Johari window model with relation to your role as either coach or mentor and reflect on the questions posed.

What insight have you gained from reflecting on the model?

Consider areas within the coaching mentoring relationship that would benefit most by using this model.

Insight Coaching & Mentoring Programme

7 – Article To Match or Mis-Match? The Dynamics of Mentoring

The Dynamics of Mentoring as a Route to Personal and Organisational Learning - Richard Hale

Here we include an article written by Dr Richard Hale which summarises the key outcomes from an extensive research project into the dynamics of mentoring relationships. This is presented here as it provides a theoretical backdrop to the subject of mentoring and links into some of the inputs and practical tools provided in subsequent Modules.

The article was first published in Career Development International 5/4/5 [2000] p 223-234.

Introduction

This paper summarises key findings from the doctoral research work of the author Richard Hale, exploring the dynamics of mentoring as a route to personal and organisational learning. This research, which is part of a research programme through International Management Centres and Southern Cross University, Australia, has been conducted using action research and grounded theory methodologies.

Presented here are the findings from 48 semi-structured interviews conducted with mentors and mentees and from 23 questionnaires. The main focus of the work has been the comparison of results from two organisationally-driven mentoring initiatives, one at Scottish Hydro-Electric and the other at Skipton Building Society. Previously reported in the Continuing Professional Development Issue 3 1999 were the initial findings concerning the research carried out at Scottish Hydro-Electric.

Conclusions drawn from the analysis so far have led to the early development of further theoretical understanding of the dynamics of the formal mentoring relationship, to the identification of further areas worthy of research and to the design of a diagnostic tool to aid the process of matching mentor and mentee.

This will be of interest to those responsible for setting up mentoring in organisations as well as individuals involved in mentoring and researchers in this field.

Matching

Arguably a key determinant of success in establishing a viable and successful relationship is that of finding a good match between the mentor and mentee. The question which follows from this is how do we define 'good' and as far as this research is concerned the focus remains clearly on whether the relationship supports and leads to learning on the part of the mentor and mentee.

In the literature a range of approaches are described in matching mentor and mentee (Black, Sweeney and Brewster, 1997; Forret *et al.*, 1996; Gaines, 1997; IDS, 1996; Tabbron *et al.* 1997; Veal & Wachtel, 1996). Some organisations will take a very laissez-faire approach and allow mentor/mentee relationships simply to evolve and then offer support to allow the relationship to hopefully flourish. Others will take a very interventionist approach, using certain criteria to match mentor with mentee and the decision regarding pairing is actually taken by a third party. Somewhere in between these extremes lies a middle ground where the third party facilitates the pairing of mentor and mentee by providing support and guidance but allowing the actual decision to be taken by the mentor and mentee.

Insight Coaching & Mentoring Programme

The IDS study (1996) identified matching as one of the major pitfalls in company mentoring schemes. Chao, Waltz and Gardner (1992) warned that care must be shown in the matching process in formal mentoring programmes:

'A current practice of random assignment of protégés to mentors is analogous to blind dates; there would be a small probability that the match would be successful, but more attention to the selection phase would raise this probability above chance levels.' (p. 634)

However despite the recognition of the need to take care when pairing mentor and mentee and the range of approaches taken, it would appear there is no evidence of a consistently reliable approach. Sometimes the best intentions of those taking the third party interventionist approach can be rejected. For instance Linda Holbeche, described in Megginson and Clutterbuck (1995), how at Roffey Park in the UK the attempt to match female mentors and mentees was rejected as patronising by men and insulting to the women. Gaines (1997) refers to how the Transport Research Laboratory used recruitment staff to manage the matching process, presumably because of an assumed better understanding of selection issues than line managers.

In their interviews with HR managers from Hallmark Cards, Texaco Trading and Transportation, Imperial Oil, Shell and a computer company, Forret et al. (1996) revealed that matching ranged from random to structured 'dating'. It is commented that:

'Although no systematic research has been performed to determine which method of pairing is best, it is probably safe to assume that using a random matching process will result in a higher percentage of mentoring relationships that might be deemed 'unsatisfactory' by both mentor and protégé. Discussions with past and potential participants in a mentoring programme should provide useful input in determining how to pair mentors and protégés.' (p28)

Consideration of the style of the mentor and the mentee and their expectations in terms of, for instance, communications and culture, were raised as important issues for consideration by Conway (1996). He noted how some people are better able to work with ambiguity than others and how some will come from a culture where leaders are expected to be omniscient - this will affect the mentee's expectations of the mentor. Conway (1998) was rather dismissive of attempts to systematise the matching process, including the use of learning styles, and he suggested that it is more appropriate to treat each case on an individual basis. He argued that what will be appropriate will depend on the needs of the individual concerned.

In considering the options when it comes to matching, Hay (1995) identified the following three factors:

1   Whether to mix or match on factors such as gender, culture, education, background and age.

2   The need for support or challenge, recognising that over time both are needed. Referring to her own model of different working styles she recognised the danger of too much similarity leading to collusion or comfort and the potential for contrasting styles to lead to learning. However she also noted the danger of too much contrast leading to irreconcilable differences.

3   Whether or not the mentor should be a role model, recognising though that the aim should not be to clone particular managerial types.

As with other writers, though, Hay identified the options and possible outcomes but did not really suggest anything more definitive than the need to be aware of the process one is using in matching and to at least decide some criteria. -

Insight Coaching & Mentoring Programme

Research by Alleman and Newman (1984), Alleman, Cochran, Doverspike and Newman (1984) and Alleman, Klein and Newman (1984) in reviewing much US based literature and apparently considering informal mentoring, identifies three possible reasons that are suggested as to why mentors select protégés. Some suggest it is to do with perceived similarity, which reduces uncertainty as both parties are able to supply missing data from their readily available self-schema. Others suggest selection is based on recognition of ability which will come from the protégé raising his or her own visibility. It may also be that the mentor has a stereotype of an effective subordinate and the mentee may have a stereotype of the effective leader which is used to support selection decisions. It is commented how the idea of selection based on contrast or complementary characteristics is only rarely mentioned in the literature. They found that what differentiates mentors from others is what they do, in other words behaviours, rather than innate qualities. Also in making one of the few comments found regarding the selection of mentees, it is suggested that they should be selected on the basis of their talent, potential, eagerness to learn and willingness to participate in mentoring. It should be noted though that there is a US theme of advancement and sponsorship running through these recommendations.

This literature confirmed the value of developing guidance that might assist the growth of effective mentoring relationships. One might reasonably expect to be able to develop behaviours and competencies through intervention rather than develop or change innate personality related qualities.

Of particular relevance to the focus on management learning, and the interest in the dynamics of mentoring which underlies this research, is the work of Honey and Mumford (1982) and Mumford (1995a, 1995b, 1995c, 1996, 1997) in the area of learning styles. A major contribution of these authors has been to provide a widely-used model of learning styles and an associated diagnostic instrument. The Honey and Mumford model suggested four styles of learning: activist, reflector, theorist and pragmatist. It was suggested that managers have preferences for certain approaches to learning over and above others, in other words a preferred learning style. Mumford proposed that the preferred learning style of the mentor and mentee are worthy of consideration when matching and will influence the dynamics of the relationship. It was suggested for instance that pragmatists will be interested in learning opportunities relevant to their job, whereas a theorist mentor could be more generalist in discussion. Essentially mentoring was seen as guiding the learner through a process of reflection, and as such activists might not make the best mentors as they will prefer to leap in with their own solutions. Mumford suggested that the mentor and learner should be introduced to the learning cycle and learning styles. He recognised that differences in style between mentor and mentee could provide strength in the relationship as far as learning is concerned, but this calls for tolerance. He reluctantly concluded that matching based on similarity was more likely to work.

There was some discussion of learning styles by Hay (1995) and in summary she suggested:

- Activist mentees may be too impatient.
- Reflector mentees will want time to review their experiences but may hold back from moving on or making decisions about action.
- Theorists will want to learn new frameworks and theories, as well as wanting to teach the mentor, but may be over analytical.
- Pragmatists generate lots of practical idea but might expect too much from the mentor by way of solutions.

Hay does not provide any empirical evidence of the effectiveness of the combination of learning styles covered by mentor and mentee. Whilst her suggestions, as outlined above, do seem to have face, it should be noted that Honey and Mumford do not suggest the individual can be characterised by one style alone.

Insight Coaching & Mentoring Programme

The researcher recognised that the subject of similarities and differences in terms of learning styles, and how this influences the mentoring relationship, was worthy of further research. It was opportune that the two main organisations participating in the research, Scottish Hydro-Electric and Skipton Building Society, had matched mentor and mentee using different criteria, namely similarity and contrast in learning style respectively.

In summary, from the literature concerning the matching process and the dynamics of the relationship, the researcher recognised that a major challenge was presented. This was to research the dynamics of mentoring relationships in relation to learning, with the aim of identifying at least some ground rules that would assist organisations in pairing mentor with mentee.

There have been valuable contributions to the literature in the areas of defining mentoring and in considering the qualities of an effective mentor. Also much has been written about the outcomes of mentoring for the individual, albeit with more emphasis on mentee than mentor outcomes. There would, however, appear to be little systematic research regarding the impact of mentoring on learning for mentee, mentor *and* the organisation. Equally there is little research regarding the impact of the dynamics of mentoring, in terms of individual similarities and differences, upon learning.

The research questions that were explored through the action research interventions are summarised as follows:

1   How does the mentoring process and relationship contribute to learning in terms of knowledge, skills and insights, for the mentee?

1. In what way does the organisation benefit from individual learning which occurs as a result of the mentoring relationship?

2. How does the mentoring process and relationship contribute to learning in terms of knowledge, skills and insights, for the mentor?

3. How do similarities and differences between the mentor and mentee influence the effectiveness of the relationship in terms of learning for both parties?

The findings related to these questions are discussed in this paper.

The Sample

Table 1 shows the research population. Interviews were conducted with mentors and mentees at separate times. At Scottish Hydro-Electric the mentees were participants in a scheme targeted at a high-potential group known as the 'developer' group. Mentors were more senior managers at least one level above the mentees. At Skipton Building Society there were two mentoring schemes. The middle management group were established managers being mentored by board level directors. The accelerate groups were high-potential graduates early in their career with mentors at middle management level.

Insight Coaching & Mentoring Programme

Table 1 - Semi-Structured Interviews Conducted With Mentors and Mentees

	Mentors	Mentees
Total	22	25
Scottish Hydro-Electric	9	9
Male	7	7
Female	1*	2
	* Inc. 1 Mentor to 2 mentees	

	Mentors	Mentees
Skipton Building Society Middle Management Group	7	10
Male	6**	4
Female	0	6
	** Inc. 1 Mentor to 2 mentees	

Skipton Building Society Accelerate to Management Group	6	6
Male	5	1
Female	1	5

Mentor and Mentee 'Dynamics of Mentoring' Questionnaires

	Mentors	Mentees
Total	13	11
Male	10	9
Female	3	2

Insight Coaching & Mentoring Programme

Key Findings

Below is a summary of the key findings as analysed from the data drawn from the research interviews.

Data was recorded using the pro-forma setup in Microsoft Word and this data was then imported into a software package designed specifically for qualitative data analysis and research, QSR NUD*IST produced by Sage Publications. This package was seen as offering help in the analysis of a high quantity of data of a qualitative nature, particularly in allowing data to be packaged and analysed in many ways. From within the QSR NUD*IST package the interviewee files were then coded in turn in order to allow subsequent analysis.

How does the mentoring process and relationship contribute to learning in terms of knowledge, skills and insights, for the mentee?

The evidence from this research suggests the real power of mentoring is in the development of insights. One should not ignore knowledge though because the effective mentor allows the mentee to make connections between knowledge and personal experience in order to develop insights.

Mentoring does lead to skills development but it depends on the extent to which the mentor takes on a 'coaching' role compared to the other roles of counsellor, networker and facilitator as described by Clutterbuck (1993). The results here confirm the suggestion of Mumford (1998) that mentoring can be a powerful way of developing mentee insights.

The findings do not support the views of Kantor (Clawson, 1985) that where there is a good mentoring relationship the individual is less likely to take steps towards skills development through training interventions. It would appear that the organisational climate in terms of supporting learning through mentoring, coaching and training interventions is more important.

Also the extent to which coaching is applied will depend on the nature of the mentoring relationship. Hay's (1995) definitions of different types of mentoring relationship are helpful here. Her definitions of traditional mentoring, where the older mentor supports the early career development of the mentee, and the master/apprentice model, fit quite well with the Scottish Hydro-Electric and Skipton Building Society schemes.

Mentoring appears to support the development in the mentee of certain behaviours and qualities that do not conveniently fit into the knowledge, skills and insights categories. These might be considered difficult to tackle through traditional off-the-job training courses and include such behaviours and qualities as risk-taking, action-orientation, self-belief and confidence.

The findings present a challenge to Clawson's (1985) comment that one should pay more attention to line management relationships rather than being so concerned with the mentoring relationship. It was seen with one very powerful example how the effective mentor was able to support the mentee in managing a difficult issue regarding the line manager relationship. In this case the mentee was in an awkward position of having to confront the fact that the line manager was asking her to do something considered unethical.

Finally it is worth noting that the development of knowledge and skills through mentoring is easier to plan for than the development of insights. Knowledge and skills are more straightforward to define and more objective, observable and testable than insights. Insights begin more with the individual and emerge for the individual, assisted by the effective mentor, and are more personal. The development of insights is less easily planned; whether or not they emerge will depend on the real-life circumstances and experiences of the mentee and the extent to which the mentor can assist the mentee to make the connection between experience and him or herself.

Emerging Theoretical Models The following model (Figure 1) is proposed as a way of understanding the how the mentee can develop insights from the mentoring relationship. Effective mentors will help mentees access their own bank of knowledge and experience and will open up access to the mentor's previously acquired knowledge and experience. Furthermore the effective mentor will help the mentee to identify current or potential experience-based opportunities to develop insights.

Figure 1 - Model for the Development of Mentee Insights

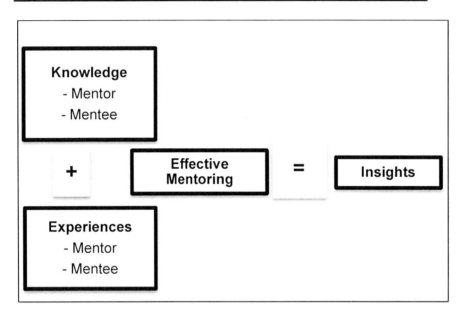

Figure 2 shows that the effective mentoring experience provides various opportunities for the development of insights. Through the top left window the mentee is able to access the views and experiences of the mentor. Through the top right window there is access to the workings of the organisation which the mentor may provide by discussing activities and strategies being addressed at a senior level. Through the bottom right window there is access to the workings of senior managers. This is slightly different to the top right window in that this is where the mentee gains an understanding of the politics and inter-personal dynamics of senior level personnel. Finally through the bottom left window the mentee achieves a level of self-insight through what is described as 'Q', or questioning, in this case 'self-questioning'. For example, the mentee may be confronted with thinking through or re-thinking his or her approach to career development, to relationships with others or to personal abilities and potential.

Insight Coaching & Mentoring Programme

Figure 2 - Windows of Insight Through Mentoring

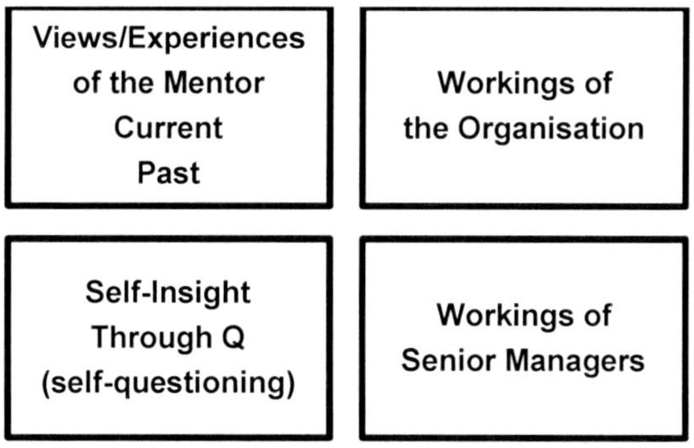

Views/Experiences of the Mentor Current Past	Workings of the Organisation
Self-Insight Through Q (self-questioning)	Workings of Senior Managers

Recommendations & Key Findings

1. Knowledge acquisition might be helped by the mentoring relationship and may be easier to plan for. It is arguably less powerful in terms of personal learning. By comparison the development of insights is a more personal and powerful learning achievement, however this is less 'plannable' and more dependent on circumstances and the dynamics of the relationship.

2. Mentoring might be seen as providing the 'missing link' between skills that can be developed through training and implementation because it helps address some of the blocks to change such as self-belief, action orientation and risk taking. Mentoring may help ensure skills development is transferred to the job and is sustainable.

3. Mentoring may help the development of confidence on the part of the mentee and this may result in more sustained changes than, say, increased confidence achieved through a short training course alone.

4. The organisation could help the mentor to support the mentee in turning knowledge into insights by explaining the difference between the two levels of learning.

5. Mentors could explore specifically with mentees how their learning is translating into action, either through discussion with the mentee or by seeking evidence through other sources (with permission of the mentee).

6. Where the culture of the organisation allows, it is useful if the mentor can take a proactive role in supporting mentee development outside of the mentoring meetings.

7. Where a trusting mentoring relationship exists the mentee may be able to call on the mentor for support when there are difficulties between the mentee and the line manager.

Insight Coaching & Mentoring Programme

8. Mentoring provides a powerful vehicle for discussing inter-personal relationships including the mentee's relationship with his or her line manager.

9. It may be beneficial to seek evidence of informal mentoring relationships with a view to supporting these rather than simply relying on the formal mentoring approach.

In what way does the organisation benefit from individual learning which occurs as a result of the mentoring relationship?

Unravelling whether a benefit of mentoring is more of an organisational or individual one is impossible, because the two are often inextricably linked and there are some cases where the individual benefits will naturally be seen as also constituting an organisational benefit. However from this research there are some examples of what might be considered organisational benefits of mentoring that support some of the claims of others as discussed in the literature. Also there are some findings that contrast with the findings or experiences of other researchers and organisations.

Lunding et al.'s (1978) experience at Jewel was that mentoring supported challenging upwards and this is also seen in the findings from this research. If not overtly mentioning challenging, certainly several mentees, particularly at Skipton Building Society, said they felt more comfortable with approaching senior managers and it **had encouraged upward communication**.

There was also evidence to support the findings of Forret *et al.* (1996) that mentoring provides access to careers advice. Furthermore mentees in some cases said the relationship had helped them to realise the importance of managing their own career in a proactive way. This could be considered as a deeper insight than simply gaining advice about a potential career path.

There was also much evidence of mentoring helping with developing an appreciation of the company culture and feeling of support as found by Forret *et al.* and the IDS study (1996).

Regarding the subject of the link with retention the IDS study had suggested links but recognised these were inconclusive whereas Alleman (1989) presented strong evidence in one scheme of a link between mentoring and retention. In the research presented here there were indeed some examples of cases at Skipton Building Society where it was considered that the effectiveness of the mentoring relationship led to retention of the mentee, who may otherwise have considered moving jobs. It should be noted, though, that in other cases at Scottish Hydro-Electric mentoring contributed to the mentee's decision to leave. In some cases this was stated by the mentee as due to the failure of the organisation to meet raised expectations and in others it was due to a realisation that there was not a good fit between the individual and the organisation.

It would be wrong to make a definitive statement about mentoring leading to improved motivation as there are so many variables that influence motivation. Also there were examples at Scottish Hydro-Electric of some mentees saying that mentoring had contributed to de-motivation due to the fact the organisation was unable to meet their expectations. In these cases this might have been prevented had the individuals realised the overall purpose of the mentoring scheme which was not primarily focused on career advancement. There was support for the findings of Conway (1996) at London Borough of Brent that mentoring improves the awareness of each other's role on the part of the mentor and mentee and for the findings of Coley (1996) who found that at Apple Computers, mentoring helped in developing business awareness, improved communications across functions and understanding of the challenges faced by the

Insight Coaching & Mentoring Programme

organisation's leaders. Also in the cases of Scottish Hydro-Electric and Skipton Building Society there was evidence of improved understanding of the informal structures and the culture of the organisation as seen in the Bass scheme and improved communication as reported from Prudential (IDS, 1996).

Recommendations & Key Findings

1.   Organisational learning and benefits are difficult to quantify, however organisations would gain from clearly stating the corporate objectives and seeking to assess progress against these goals.

2.   It is important to manage the expectations of mentees appropriately when setting up mentoring. There is a need to integrate other development processes, such as career development planning, training, succession planning and systems with mentoring.

3.   Successful mentoring schemes, set up at the right time in the organisation's development, may support the improvement of upward and downward communication. Mentoring can open up communication in many directions: upwards as mentees become more comfortable communicating with seniors downwards as mentors improve their awareness of different parts of the organisation and across the organisation where mentees and mentors come together for group reviews.

4.   Mentoring relationships, if trusting and open, can help address problems between the mentee and the line manager.

5.   Mentoring can help retention of key personnel through both the specific support given and the demonstration of commitment from a senior level.

6.   Mentoring can support the development of key skills throughout the organisation, particularly where the mentor takes on a coaching role as part of mentoring.

How does the mentoring process and relationship contribute to learning in terms of knowledge, skills and insights, for the mentor?

Several writers have suggested mentoring helps meet the mentors needs for generativity, in other words the need for passing on one's wisdom to future generations (Clawson, 1996; Levinson et al., 1978; Scandura, 1996) however in this research there is limited evidence of this. In most cases when mentors were asked about their objectives in entering the relationship the answer was either that they did not have any, or they made somewhat bland 'motherhood' statements such as wanting to help the organisation's effort. In most cases it might be considered that mentors were still in the prime of their own career or had further potential to achieve and given the fact that the organisation was driving the mentoring initiative, the generativity argument is weak. A small minority of mentors referred to their satisfaction in being able to pass on their wisdom to younger members of the organisation. So it may be that the generativity motive on the part of the mentor is stronger in informal or unassigned relationships where the mentor falls more naturally into a mentoring relationship of his or her choice. Perhaps more appropriate in the case of the organizationally-driven mentoring relationships studied in this research would be the concept of social exchange theory, whereby the mentor partakes, knowing that there is likely to be some benefit in return. Such benefits might be for instance being seen as supportive of organisational initiatives and being recognised as a mentoring manager. Mentoring clearly can provide learning opportunities for the mentor and this is a point stressed by Clutterbuck (1995). Overall there was evidence of learning on the part of the mentor but one could not help but think there were missed opportunities too.

Insight Coaching & Mentoring Programme

The learning benefits that were described by the mentor fall into the following broad categories:

- Reflection on their own development needs, prompted by encouraging the mentee to address the same issue.
- Refreshment of their own skills through having to coach or guide the mentee.
- Appreciation of the role of the mentee and his or her part of the business.
- Development of their own style of management through experimentation in the role of mentor.
- Insight into how they were perceived by others in the business.

An interesting comment was made by one mentor who felt that too much openness with the mentee regarding his own development needs and learning might lead to him losing respect. This suggests the individual placed much importance on being seen as an authority figure with a degree of 'power distance' as described by Hofstede (1991). It also suggests that the extent to which this individual was able to learn, through for instance discussion and feedback from the mentee, was restricted due to an unwillingness or inability to self-disclose. It is the process of self-disclosure which leads to reciprocation on the part of the other party. This leads to more open communication, giving and receiving of feedback, development of trust and learning as the individuals move towards the achievement of their potential (Hale and Whitlam, 1999).

Recommendations & Key Findings

- There is potential for organisations to focus more attention on the learning objectives and outcomes of the mentor.
- Convening mentors to discuss their experiences could provide valuable support.
- It may help the mentee if the mentor is able to describe his/her own objectives and what s/he is gaining from the relationship, however this calls for a level of openness and disclosure on the part of the mentor.
- Mentors may gain insights into their own line management style through the experience of mentoring. Mentoring provides mentors with the opportunity to develop a 'mentoring' style of management.
- Mentoring can refresh management skills by raising awareness of prior learning.
- It may help both mentor and mentee for mentors to discuss their own learning with the mentee. The mentor may gain from reflecting on and articulating personal learning and for the mentee such openness may build trust and rapport. However, willingness to do this may be influenced by the enthusiasm of the mentor to disclose in what may be seen as a senior role compared to the mentee.

How do similarities and differences between the mentor and mentee influence the effectiveness of the relationship in terms of learning for both parties?

In both organisations job movement was frequent and as posited by Kram (1985) it could be seen that the cultivation stage of the relationship was reached quicker than her suggested norm of two to five years. Also as the organisations studied had established formal or assigned mentoring relationships as part of an organisational scheme, it might be expected that there was a focus on developing the relationship quicker, yet a realistic expectation that the depth of the relationship will be shallower than the best of the informal relationships as researched by for instance Kram (1985) and Levinson et al (1978).

Insight Coaching & Mentoring Programme

As far as developing the relationship successfully is concerned the challenge for organisations seems to be to ensure there is a match in terms of similar values and belief structures on the part of mentor and mentee. If there was a way of assessing such characteristics prior to matching mentor and mentee this could help improve the chances of obtaining a sustainable match.

Kram's (1985) observations, that the extent to which the culture of the organisation encourages self-disclosure and openness and the importance of relationships are relevant. Where mentors and mentees engaged in self-disclosure this helped in the development of trust whereas lack of disclosure led to more superficial and less personal relationships.

The various concerns of Kram regarding the nature of cross-gender relationships were not, however, supported. She said males and females revert to stereotype roles and that others may see the relationship as one of intimacy and favouritism. These concerns were not discussed in this research and this may have been helped by the fact that the relationships were formally assigned as part of an organisation-wide mentoring initiative.

Kram's concern that hierarchy can inhibit the mentee was given some credence by those who were matched with mentors more than one level up describing their apprehension at first. However the evidence suggests with careful handling and sensitivity on the part of the mentor this can be overcome.

Age would appear from this research to be less of an issue than suggested by Levinson et al. (1978) and Mendleson et al. (1989). Overall mentees seem more concerned that they should respect the mentor for his or her achievement and experience rather than age per se, constituting a criterion for judgement. It should be noted though that the participants by and large came from achievement oriented culture, rather than ascriptive ones as defined by Trompenaars (1993) where value is given to people's experience. This might be different in more ascriptive cultures where value is ascribed to others based on age, which is usually correlated with status.

There is support for the views of Hay (1995) that too much similarity of working style may lead to comfort rather than learning challenge but that too much contrast can lead to irreconcilable differences. In the cases where individuals felt there was too much contrast in values and beliefs, one party would simply allow the relationship to falter rather than confronting the other party.

It is proposed that when seeking to match mentor and mentee it is helpful to consider similarities and differences across a range of criteria. Clearly an overriding consideration will be 'what are the objectives in setting up the mentoring relationship?' If the aim is primarily to facilitate learning for the mentee then different criteria may be identified than, for instance, if an important objective is to facilitate mentor learning. Also it will be necessary to consider whether the mentee is ready and willing to work with a more challenging and confronting mentor who may be quite different in style or whether a more comfortable but less challenging relationship is appropriate.

Insight Coaching & Mentoring Programme

Having said all of this the models below show the impact of similarities and differences as identified through the research. It can be seen in Figure 3 that if the aim is to speed the development of the relationship then an important consideration will be to seek similarities in terms of, for instance interests, academic of professional background or even family circumstances. Mentees in the research were quite clear in stating that these factors helped speed the development of rapport and trust.

In Figure 4 it is shown that if the aim is to optimise learning for the mentee and possibly the mentor then there is a need to look for contrasts in terms of, for instance, personal style, learning style, strengths and development needs. However one should seek some similarity in terms of overall values, beliefs and life goals. The research showed clearly that, where relationships failed most dramatically in terms of learning and sustainability, this was attributed by both mentors and mentees to fundamental differences at this level.

Figure 3 – Speeding the Development of the Relationship

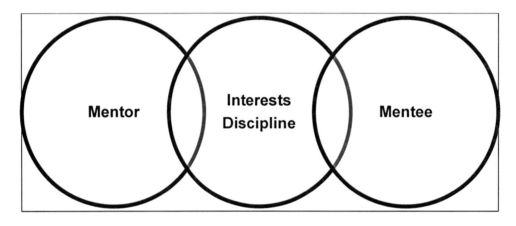

Figure 4 – Optimising Learning

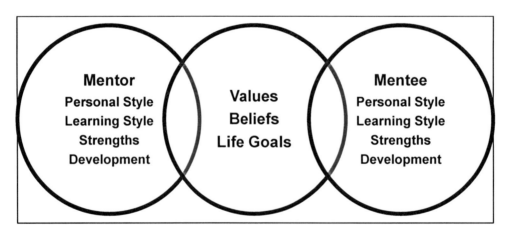

Insight Coaching & Mentoring Programme

Recommendations & Key Findings

1. When matching mentor and mentee if possible seek to understand some of the fundamental values of both parties to ensure there is no obvious clash, as this is likely to hinder the relationship.

2. Mentoring relationships where the mentor is one level up from the mentee are likely to lead to quicker development. Where the mentor is more than one level up, more time should be made available for developing rapport.

3. Considering development needs of the mentee and the matching with mentors who have strengths in the relevant area may help.

4. Understanding learning styles and using the model of learning style preferences may be more important than seeking a match or contrast based on profiles.

5. Mentors and mentees should be encouraged to discuss similarities in experience and style early on in the relationship in order to encourage rapport building.

6. If mentoring is set up in a climate of supposed meritocracy then mentors with incompatible attitudes should not be matched with ambitious mentees.

7. Views regarding the gender of the mentor and mentee vary and may be dependent on personal preference and influenced by personal experiences and culture. Mentees, rather than mentors, are likely to have differing personal preferences regarding the gender of the other party.

8. Whereas some researchers have suggested a need for a certain age difference, it appears experience is actually more important. It may be that gaining experience is less dependent on age than it has been in the past.

9. Leaving too much responsibility on the mentee to set up meetings may not work where there is a difference in levels.

10. Similarities in social style may help in building rapport and similarity in basic values may make the relationship sustainable. However, too much similarity of approach and viewpoint may not support learning. Also similarity may lead to informality, which may lead to lack of structure in mentoring meetings. Further consideration should be given to the dimensions of style and values and the impact of these factors of learning.

In conclusion, it can be seen from this research that, while it may not be possible to develop a clear-cut formula to inform the matching of mentor and mentee, there are certain considerations which will help the chances of learning, potentially for both parties. Those responsible for matching, whether a third party or the actors in the relationship should consider whether similarities or differences will help and overall it is suggested that a degree of contrast will support learning, though too much will make the relationship unviable. However a key determinant of success will be the extent to which the mentor and mentee are able to tolerate differences, particularly those relating to personal values and beliefs. Equally it is important for there to be meetings that periodically review the process factors of the relationship. Where mentoring does work well it can clearly support learning at a deeper level than simply knowledge or skills; it is quite possible to help in the development of insights.

Many questions about the dynamics of the mentoring relationship remain unanswered and opportunities for further research exist, particularly in exploring the significance and impact of personal values and in studying how learning leads to insights in more depth.

Insight Coaching & Mentoring Programme

Consider the Article – 'To Match or Mis-Match?' The Dynamics of Mentoring as a Route to Personal and Organisational Learning by Richard Hale 2000.

What were the emerging themes for the:

- *Mentee*

- *Mentor*

- *Organisation*

Pause for thought and consider how you might utilize the information presented to inform your role as the mentor or indeed mentee.

Insight Coaching & Mentoring Programme

8 – Personal Reflections and Learning

In this section we encourage you to make some notes reflecting on your overall learning from completion of this module. We have structured this around the model of reflection encouraged by Boud (1985).

WHAT... have you learnt? (Review the workbook and consider learning relating to your reflections within your own practice or organisation)	SO WHAT? (Consider how your learning may have provoked you to think or plan to do things differently)	NOW WHAT? (Identify any actions you plan to take to implement your learning; try to be as specific as possible)

Insight Coaching & Mentoring Programme

References

ALLEMAN, E., 'Two Planned Mentoring Programs That Worked', *Mentoring International,* 3, No.1, 1989, pp. 6-12.

ALLEMAN, E. and NEWMAN, I., 'Interpersonal Perceptions in Mentoring Relationships', *Paper Presented to American Educational Research Association Meeting,* New Orleans, 1984.

ALLEMAN, E., COCHRAN, J., DOVERSPIKE, J. and NEWMAN, I., 'Enriching Mentoring Relationships', *The Personnel and Guidance Journal.,* February, 1984, pp. 329-331.

ALLEMAN, E., KLEIN, D., and NEWMAN, I., 'Practical Application of Research on Mentoring Relationships', *Paper Presented to The Academy of Management 44th Annual Meeting,* Boston, 1984.

BENNETTS, C., 'The Secrets of a Good Relationship', *People Management,* 29 June, 1995, pp. 38-39.

BLACK, A., SWEENEY, J. and BREWSTER, M., 'Mentoring as a Vital Component for Individuals', *Proceedings of the Fourth European Mentoring Conference,* 6th-7th November, 1997, pp.15-30.

BLOCH, S., 'Business Mentoring and Coaching', *Training and Development,* April, 1993, pp. 26-29.

BLUNT, N., 'Learning From the Wisdom of Others', *People Management,* 31 May, 1995, pp. 38-39.

CHAO, G.T., WALZ, P.M. and GARDNER, P.D., 'Formal and Informal Mentorships: A Comparison on Mentoring Functions and Contrast With Nonmentored Counterparts', *Personnel Psychology,* 45, 1992, pp. 619-636.

CLAWSON, J.G., 'Is Mentoring Necessary?', *Training & Development Journal,* April, 1985, pp. 36-39.

CLUTTERBUCK, D., *Everyone Needs a Mentor,* Institute of Personnel Management, London, 1993.

COLEY, D.B., 'Mentoring Two-by-Two', *Training & Development,* July,1996, pp.46-48.

COLLIN, A., 'Mentoring', *ICT,* March/April, 1998, pp. 23-27.

CONWAY, C., 'Mentoring to Diversity', *Directions - The Ashridge Journal,* March, 1996, pp. 21-23.

CONWAY, C., *Strategies For Mentoring,* Wiley, Chichester, 1998.

FORRET, M.L., TURBAN, D.B. and DOUGHERTY, T.W., 'Issues Facing Organizations When Implementing Formal Mentoring Programmes', *Leadership and Organization Development Journal,* 17/3, 1996.

GAINES, D., 'Mentoring - Implementation and Enhancement of the TRL Scheme', *Organisations and People,* 4.4, 1997, pp. 26-29.

HALE, R. and WHITLAM.P., *Impact, Impressions and Influence,* Kogan Page, London, 1999.

HAY, J., *Transformational Mentoring,* McGraw-Hill, London, 1995.

HOFMEYR, K.B., 'Can Mentorship be Institutionalised?', *IPM Journal,* , April, 1987, pp. 13-15.

HOFSTEDE, G., *Cultures and Organizations: Software of the mind.,* McGraw-Hill, London, 1991.

HONEY, P. and MUMFORD, A., *The Manual of Learning Styles,* Honey, 1982.

Incomes Data Services, *Mentoring Schemes,* IDS Study 613, November, 1996.

KRAM, K.E., *Mentoring at Work: Developmental Relationships in Organisational Life,* Scott, Foresman, Glenview, IL, 1985.

KRAM, K. and HALL, D., 'Mentoring as an Antidote to Stress During Corporate Trauma', *Human Resource Management,* 28, No. 4, 1991, pp. 493-510.

LEVINSON, D.J., DARROW, C.N., KLEIN, E.B., LEVINSON, M.A. and McKEE, B., *The Season's of a Man's Life,* Knopf, New York, 1978.

Insight Coaching & Mentoring Programme

LUNDING, F.J., CLEMENTS, G.L., and PERKINS, D.S., 'Everyone Who Makes It Has a Mentor', *Harvard Business Review,* July-August , 1978, pp. 89-101.

MEGGINSON, D. and CLUTTERBUCK, D., *Mentoring in Action,* Kogan Page, London, 1995

MENDLESON, J.L., BARNES, A.K. and HORN, G., 'The Guiding Light to Corporate Culture', *Personnel Administrator,* July1989, pp.70-72.

MUMFORD, A., 'Creating a Learning Environment', *Croner, Journal of Professional HRM,* 4, July, 1996, pp. 26-30.

MUMFORD, A., 'Frameworks for Choice of Management Development Methods', *Author's Own Paper,* 1997.

MUMFORD, A., 'How Managers Help with Development', *Industrial & Commercial Training,* 27, No. 8, 1995b, pp.8-11.

MUMFORD, A., 'Learning Styles and Mentoring', *Industrial & Commercial Training,* 27, No. 8, 1995a, pp. 4-7

MUMFORD, A., 'Managers Developing Others Through Action Learning', *Industrial & Commercial Training,* 27, No. 2, 1995c, pp. 19-27.

MUMFORD, A., 'Sources for Courses', *People Management,*14th May, 1998a, pp. 48-50
Management Review, 22, No. 2, 1997, pp. 482-521.

SCANDURA, T.A., TEJEDA, M.J., WERTHER, W.B. and LANKAU, M.J, 'Perspectives on Mentoring', *Leadership and Organization Development Journal,* 17, No. 3, 1996, p. 50-56.

STEAD, R., 'Mentoring Young Learners: Does Everyone Really Need A Mentor', *Education and Training,* 39, No. 6, 1997, pp. 219-224.

TABBRON, A., MACAULAY, S. and COOK, S., 'Making Mentoring Work', *Training for Quality,* 5, No 1, 1997, pp. 6-9.

TROMPENAARS, F., *Riding the Waves of Culture,* Nicholas Brealey, London, 1993.

VEALE, D.J.,WACHTEL, J.M., 'Mentoring and Coaching as Part of a Human Resource Development Strategy: an example at Coca-Cola Foods', *Management Development Review,* 9, 6, 1996, pp.16-20.

Additional Resources

Luft, J.; Ingham, H. (1950). "The Johari window, a graphic model of interpersonal awareness". *Proceedings of the western training laboratory in group development* (Los Angeles: UCLA).

Luft, J. (1969). *Of Human Interaction.* Palo Alto, CA: National Press. pp. 177.

Luft, J. (1972). *Einfuhrung in die Gruppendynamik.* Klett.

Handy, C. (2000). *21 Ideas for Managers.* San Francisco: Jossey-Bass.

Insight Coaching & Mentoring Programme

The Insight series continues with 2 additional workbooks

Insight Coaching & Mentoring Programme
Dr Richard Hale and Eileen Hutchinson

Workbook 2 "Assessing Capability"

Assessing Capability is a 70 page workbook which provides practical tools backed up by research and theory to support the role of the coach or mentor in working with learners who need to develop awareness of capabilities, development needs and potential.

This workbook will enable you to:

- Describe the key competencies required of an effective coach and mentor
- Consider your own strengths and development needs as a coach and mentor against these competencies
- Self-assess your capability in working as a group coach with an action learning set
- Use the Skills and Behaviour Analysis Questionnaire to support your coaching and mentoring activities and identify strengths and development needs of coachees and mentees.
- Provide guidance on activities to support the development of skills and behaviours identified through application of the Skills and Behaviour Analysis Questionnaire.
- Use your knowledge of learning style preferences in order to support coaching and mentoring relationships.

Workbook 3 "Impact, Influence and NLP"

Impact Influence and NLP is a 70 page workbook which brings you the tools of impact and influence as originally developed and published by Dr Richard Hale combined with the practical techniques of NLP taught by Eileen Hutchinson. This provides an excellent toolkit for coaches and mentors to use when supporting their learners as well as being relevant for their own development.

This workbook will enable you to:

- Understand your sources of power and influence and that of others
- Use a structured approach when preparing to influence others
- Apply the Hale Circle of Influence
- Work with the key competencies of influencing and persuasion
- Develop strategies for managing confrontation effectively
- Manage the impression others form of you
- Implement key techniques and tools of NLP
- Expand your comfort zone and levels of personal self confidence

Insight Coaching & Mentoring Programme

Further training courses and consultancy in Coaching and Mentoring, NLP, Leadership and related topics, including for example;

Coaching and Mentoring
Would you like to improve your coaching and mentoring skills? You may have an interest in developing others to be coaches and mentors in the workplace, or perhaps you are a manager in an organisation or an employed or freelance coach or mentor. We run ILM level 3, 5 or 7 coaching and mentoring accredited courses.

Introduction to NLP for business – A 2 day interactive course covering the foundations of NLP and how it can benefit both you and your business.

NLP Coaching & Mentoring accredited course – Modular NLP coaching courses covering the NLP practitioner curriculum. NLP can help you with confidence levels, self esteem and specific work related skills, such as improving your professional style, communications, motivation, to forming and improving relationships, and more importantly to have a fuller understanding of your unique skill and abilities.

NLP Leadership – The course is aimed at experienced professionals who wish to develop their skills in the practice of NLP (Neuro Linguistic Programming), this programme will enhance your leadership role and style within the workplace. Accredited and Endorsed by ILM institute of Leadership and Management.

Impact and Influence – This course provides a practical introduction to the tools and techniques of successful influencing as developed by Dr Richard Hale with his research, publications all underpinned by the Hale Circle of Influence. This is relevant whether you are training others in the skills of influence or seeking to develop your own capability and self confidence.

Action Learning Facilitator Accreditation -Introducing the skills and know-how to apply work based action learning in your or your clients' organisations. Based on proven methods for making action learning work and linking learning with business strategies. A two day workshop followed by application and accreditation at postgraduate level over three months. ILM endorsed.

More advanced courses are also available – In company training is tailored to meet the needs of your organisation. We also offer one-to-one high performance coaching.

As developed by Eileen Hutchinson.

For further details or an informal chat please call me on 01438 310074 or 07771825030

Email Eileen.hutchinson@talktalk.net www.eileenhutchinson.com

Email info@hcma.me.uk www.hcma.me.uk

Email rhale@viprojects.com http://richardhale-learninginaction.blogspot.com/

Lightning Source UK Ltd.
Milton Keynes UK
UKOW012153210212

187694UK00001B/1/P